BTEC First ICT Practitioners

Core units and selected specialist units for the BTEC First Certificate and Diploma for ICT Practitioners

D0480770

endorsed by
edexcel ⣿

This material has been endorsed by Edexcel and offers high quality support for the delivery of Edexcel qualifications.

Edexcel endorsement does not mean that this material is essential to achieve any Edexcel qualification, nor does it mean that this is the only suitable material available to support any Edexcel qualification. No endorsed material will be used verbatim in setting any Edexcel examination and any resource lists produced by Edexcel shall include this and other appropriate texts. While this material has been through an Edexcel quality assurance process, all responsibility for the content remains with the publisher.

Copies of official specifications for all Edexcel qualifications may be found on the Edexcel website – www.edexcel.org.uk

BTEC First ICT Practitioners
Core units and selected specialist units for the BTEC First Certificate and Diploma for ICT Practitioners

Sharon Yull

endorsed by
edexcel

ELSEVIER

AMSTERDAM • BOSTON • HEIDELBERG • LONDON • NEW YORK • OXFORD
PARIS • SAN DIEGO • SAN FRANCISCO • SINGAPORE • SYDNEY • TOKYO
Newnes is an imprint of Elsevier

Newnes

004 YUL TS3S36

Newnes is an imprint of Elsevier
Linacre House, Jordan Hill, Oxford OX2 8DP
30 Corporate Drive, Burlington, MA 01803

First published 2007

Copyright © 2007, Sharon Yull. Published by Elsevier Ltd. All rights reserved

The right of Sharon Yull to be identified as the author of this work has been
asserted in accordance with the Copyright, Designs and Patents Act 1988

No part of this publication may be reproduced in any material form (including photocopying or
storing in any medium by electronic means and whether or not transiently or incidentally to
some other use of this publication) without the written permission of the copyright holder
except in accordance with the provisions of the Copyright, Designs and Patents Act 1988 or
under the terms of a licence issued by the Copyright Licensing Agency Ltd, 90 Tottenham Court
Road, London, England W1T 4LP. Applications for the copyright holder's written permission to
reproduce any part of this publication should be addressed to the publisher

Permissions may be sought directly from Elsevier's Science and Technology Rights Department
in Oxford, UK: phone: (+44) (0) 1865 843830; fax: (+44) (0) 1865 853333;
e-mail: permissions@elsevier.co.uk. You may also complete your request on-line via the Elsevier
homepage (http://www.elsevier.com), by selecting 'Customer Support' and then 'Obtaining
Permissions'

British Library Cataloguing in Publication Data
A catalogue record for this book is available from the British Library

Library of Congress Cataloguing in Publication Data
A catalogue record for this book is available from the Library of Congress

ISBN: 978-0-7506-8324-1

For information on all Newnes publications
visit our web site at www.newnespress.com

Printed and bound in Italy

07 08 09 10   10 9 8 7 6 5 4 3 2 1

Working together to grow
libraries in developing countries

www.elsevier.com | www.bookaid.org | www.sabre.org

ELSEVIER   BOOK AID International   Sabre Foundation

'To my dad, I miss you everyday'

Contents

Note from the author

Isn't it funny how life unfolds, it wasn't so long ago that I was in detention for some misdemeanour at school. After being told that I would never really amount to much and discouraged to stay on and do A' levels by my teachers, I thought 'I'll show you', and at this stage in my life, I now feel that I have.

Forever the pragmatist, I always believe that things happen for a reason and that your life is mapped out for you from beginning to end; and although I have images of grandeur, fame and worldwide recognition – the next bestselling author, dramatised in two parts on television and film, I remain convinced that my contribution although not on global life-changing scale will make a difference.

And so my message to you is always aim high, be realistic in your goals, remain optimistic of what the future will bring and be in charge of your own destiny.

Don't look back on your life and regret the things that you haven't done, look back fondly and reflect on the things that you have.

To my mother, husband and daughter the best things in my life.

Sharon Yull

Adding author to my list of achievements features quite highly on my list. Although I have contributed to a range of publications in the past, writing a complete book is something that I have wanted to do for a long time, but timing and circumstances have dictated otherwise.

I felt that I could not write a book without understanding the context of FE and ICT qualifications, therefore one of my other roles in life is that of Senior Lecturer at a large FE and HE college. Being a practitioner, for over 10 years has provided me with a range of skills and a certain level of understanding of the education arena that I have applied to other aspects in my working life.

In addition to being a practitioner, I have also acted as an educational consultant for Edexcel, LSDA and QCA and I still remain heavily involved with Edexcel in my role as Senior Subject Examiner for Higher Nationals in Computing.

Finally as if I wasn't wearing enough hats, I am also the Director of The Training and Education Company that was set-up to provide support in the form of materials, training and conferences to Centres across the country offering ICT and computing qualifications at all levels of the NQF framework.

So what else do I do, my greatest achievement is being a mother and to me the most rewarding, challenging, dynamic and fulfilling job role that I could ever add to my CV.

Preface

Welcome to the ever-changing world of information and communications technology. This book has been designed to provide you with a range of information, knowledge and skills that will facilitate you in understanding the BTEC First in ICT qualification and assessment requirements.

About you

The BTEC First in ICT qualification has been designed to provide you with a range of practical skills and underpinning knowledge that will allow you to progress onto a higher level course or prepare you for a job in ICT.

ICT is such a growing area that you will find all areas of the BTEC specification appropriate. You will be able to use elements of the qualification in a range of situations, whether it is designing a website for you or a family member, using graphics to create a dynamic document, setting up and customising a range of hardware and software or just being aware of the role and impact that ICT has on society.

You do not have to have an extensive knowledge of ICT to embark on the BTEC First qualification. Each of the units provides a good coverage of the subject matter. In conjunction, this accompanying book provides additional support in terms of a range of activities, case studies and test your knowledge sections alongside more comprehensive information that follows the guidelines of the specification.

ICT is dynamic, innovative, colourful, creative and state-of-the-art, by studying a BTEC First in ICT, a world of opportunities will present themselves, all you need to do is reach out and grab them.

About the BTEC First awards in ICT

The range of units available on the BTEC First ICT qualification is quite diverse. The units provide opportunities for you to study at a very specialist level, focussing on hardware support and fault diagnosis or graphics and web-based areas or more general applications software or business type units.

On successful completion of this qualification, the progression opportunities are quite varied, you could continue in Further Education and progress onto the GCE in Computing, GCE in Applied ICT or the National Certificate or National Diploma qualifications. Alternatively, you could apply for jobs in the areas of hardware support, web design, programming, end user support or other roles that have a business or ICT element.

The BTEC First award is an NQF Level 2 qualification and is offered at two levels, the BTEC First Certificate and the BTEC First Diploma. The Certificate is based on 180 guided learning hours and the Diploma is based on 360 guided learning hours. The qualification is composed of a range of core and specialist units. In addition, there are a range of embedded vendor qualifications such as Microsoft, CompTIA and Cisco.

Unit details	Link
Unit 1: Using ICT to Present Information	Wordprocessing Software (NVQ IT Users) Presentation Software (NVQ IT Users) Make Selective Use of IT (NVQ IT Users)
Unit 2 Introduction to Computer Systems	Operate a Computer (NVQ IT Users) Working with ICT Hardware and Equipment Level 2 (NVQ IT Practitioner)
Unit 4: Website Development	Website Software (NVQ IT Users)
Unit 6: Networking Essentials	System Operation Level 2 (NVQ IT Practitioner)
Unit 9: Database Software	Data Analysis and Data Structure Design (NVQ IT Practitioner) Database Software (NVQ IT Users)
Unit 10: Spreadsheet Software	Spreadsheet Software (NVQ IT Users)
Unit 18: ICT Graphics	Artwork and Imaging Software Level 2 (NVQ IT Users)

Links to National Occupational Standards

How to use this book

This book provides a support mechanism for the BTEC First in ICT specifications. A range of core and specialist chapters have been covered within the text, each chapter providing a range of additional materials, activities, case studies and test your knowledge sections.

Each chapter begins with an overview of the content of the related unit and addresses the learning outcomes. Following on from this, each of the main headings provides detailed coverage of the learning outcomes.

The activities have been designed to establish your level of learning and provide further opportunities for you to develop your understanding of a specific topic area or concept. The activities are devised to be used at an 'individual', 'group' or 'practical' level. The activities are broken down into a range of tasks that require you to undertake research, develop an understanding, provide an opinion, carry out an activity, discuss and present information.

The test your knowledge sections usually occur at the end of a given section and provide students with an opportunity to re-visit and refresh their understanding of a previous topic.

In some areas of the book, certain terminology is used that you may be unfamiliar with. To support your understanding of this, sections identified as 'what does this mean?' have been included that provides clarification or a definition of the terms referred to.

In conjunction to the core units – Unit 1, Using ICT to present information and Unit 2, Introduction to computer systems, five of the specialist Units have also been included. These cover, Unit 4, Website development, Unit 6 Networking essentials, Unit 9 Database software, Unit 10 Spreadsheet software and Unit 18 ICT graphics. Units 9 and 10 are smaller in length as these have been included as additional information to boost your applications-based skills.

Finally, I hope that you enjoy the content and layout of the text as this has been written with you in mind and good luck in your chosen ICT pathway and career.

Chapter 1

Using ICT to present information

This chapter will provide you with the knowledge and a range of skills that will enable you to understand the use and presentation of information in different formats. The presentation of information can be aided by the use of ICT and applications software, therefore this unit will also address what tools and techniques can support you in producing a range of documents that include examples of text, graphics and also presentation material.

Throughout this chapter you will also be able to demonstrate your ability to produce a range of different documents that can be used on a formal or informal basis such as letters, reports and other business documents.

When you complete this chapter you should be able to:

(1) Understand the purpose of different document types
(2) Understand the basis for selecting appropriate software to present and communicate information
(3) Be able to use commonly available tools and techniques in application packages
(4) Be able to review and adjust finished documents.

Different types of documents

Documents can be presented in all sorts of layouts and can be designed to suit a range of different purposes and audiences. Documents can be broken down into a number of different categories to include:

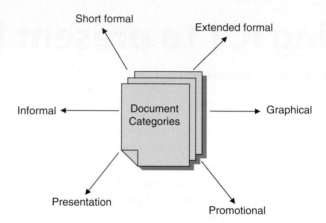

Figure 1.1
Document categories

(a) Short formal e.g. memo, e-mail, letter, order form, invoice, agenda and minutes, etc.
(b) Extended formal e.g. articles, newsletter, report, user guide
(c) Graphical documents e.g. illustrations, charts, flowcharts, diagrams
(d) Promotional e.g. advertisements, leaflets, web page
(e) Presentation e.g. electronic presentation and slide materials
(f) Informal documents e.g. texting and creative writing.

Each category can be used to suit a number of different audiences and purposes to include documents that are used in a business, at school/college or at home.

Documents have their own identity and most are easily recognisable due to their standard format. The standard format is the way in which a document is set out – how it looks.

Short formal document formats

Memorandum

Memos are used internally within an organisation, they are an informal way of communicating and documenting data and information, a template of which can be seen in Figure 1.2.

Memorandum

To: Craig Browne
From: Stewart Humphries
CC: Accounts Department
Date: 2 March 2006
Re: Late payments

Body of text would be displayed here

Figure 1.2

Memorandum template

E-mail

E-mails are now one of the most common forms or written communication. It has become one of the fastest and widely accessible formats of communication over recent years. The ability to send and receive messages has gone beyond the extent of having to sit down in front of a computer terminal and tap commands into a keyboard. New and more portable tools have become available, examples include games consoles, WAP phones, digital televisions and set-top boxes.

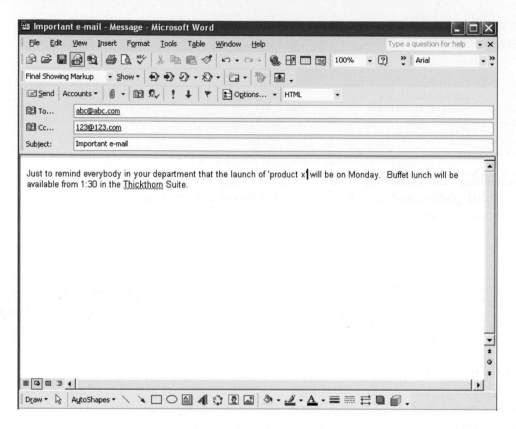

Figure 1.3

Sample e-mail

The advantages of using e-mail include:

- Speed: the ability to send messages asynchronously at the touch of the button anywhere in the world
- Multiple sends and copies: the ability to communicate the same message to multiple users
- Cost: minimal costs and depending upon the environment of use possibly no cost (if sent within an educational environment)
- Convenience: ability to communicate 24 h a day, 7 days a week
- Sharing data: because information can be transferred to multiple users, these users will have access to the same shared information that can include attached files, graphics and moving images
- Ease of use: once familiar with some of the basic functions of an e-mail package it is very easy and user friendly (because it is icon driven) to send and receive e-mail.

There are a number of other benefits of having and using e-mail in that users can keep a historical record (audit) of messages that have been sent and received. Messages can be saved into different formats, updated and printed out if required. E-mail also has a range of multimedia components that allows users to send messages containing graphics, sound, moving images and even hyperlinks to Internet pages.

The disadvantages of having and using e-mail mainly focus on technical and security issues such as:

- Spamming: the receiving of unwanted messages by advertisers, third parties and unknown users that broadcast messages universally to an entire address book
- Routing: e-mail is not always sent directly from A to B, it can be routed to other destinations before it finally reaches the receiver/s. Routing can cause a number of problems including:
  - more time is taken before the message reaches its destination
  - more opportunities for the message to be breached and intercepted by a third party
  - message can become distorted or lost.
- Security: e-mail can be intercepted easily unless some sort of encryption has been applied to the message
- Confidentiality: because e-mail can get lost, intercepted or distorted it is not deemed appropriate to send confidential messages using this format.

Letter

Different written documents have different styles and layouts each having a set of essential criteria that makes the document unique. Sometimes information has to be positioned in a specific place such as a reference, signature, date or address. An example of these can be seen in the letter template.

A letter has a number of key characteristics of which can be broken down into four main areas:

(1) An identifier
(2) Introduction
(3) The content
(4) The closure

The identifier includes items such as the sender and the recipient details such as name and address, the date, any reference codes and identification of who the letter is for.

Mr James Pearson
46 Crescent Avenue
Little Hampton
Norfolk NR33 6DL

Mr Graham Green
100 Acres Cottage
Dunnington
Suffolk
IP2 5TL

21 April 2006
Reference: BC112/00P13

Dear Mrs Green

Figure 1.4
Identifiers within a letter

The introduction should provide a short overview as to the content and also set the tone for the remainder of the letter.

Application to join the East Anglia Interactive Computing Group

After reading the advertisement in 'Buzz Computing' I would like to subscribe for a twelve month period to your interactive computing group.

Figure 1.5
Introducing a letter

The content of the letter should contain the bulk of the information. The content should be set out clearly and specifically, ensuring that the subject matter is factual and relevant to the audience.

Your advertisement in Buzz Computing on 17 January Reference: BC112/00P13 invited applications from keen gaming players to subscribe to a new computer interactive group being set up in East Anglia.

My interest in computers and games consoles has increased over the last year with me acquiring a number of rare games consoles and software, which can be considered as 'retro' items. I also enjoy interactive on-line adventure gaming sessions.

I feel that I could contribute to your group in a number of ways. I have an extensive knowledge of hardware and software. I am a keen programmer and a software enthusiast. I enclose a cheque for £85.00 for a year's subscription to your computing group, and I hope that you accept my application.

Figure 1.6
Contents of a letter

The closure section focuses on signing off the letter, and informing the recipient of any other documents that are also being sent. The recipient will expect additional documents if Enc. (Enclosure) appears at the end of the letter. In this example the additional information will be the £85.00 cheque.

Yours faithfully

James Pearson
Computing Enthusiast

Enc.

Figure 1.7

Closing a letter

Senders Information

Mrs Penelope Jordan
56 Briers
Cranburn Road
Norwich
NR7 3DD

If there is no letterhead the address could go to the right hand margin:

Mrs Penelope Jordan
56 Briers
Cranburn Road
Norwich
NR7 3DD

Recipient Information

SJ Archaeological Group
445 The Glades
Hingham Road
Norwich
NR3 3RD

Date
22 February 2006

Reference Number: (if applicable)

Salutation: For the attention of Customer Enquiry Department

Introduction: Discovery of Roman Coin circa. 66 AD

Content:

Closure:

Yours faithfully

Penelope Jordan

Figure 1.8

Complete letter template

Invoice

Invoices are written or computer generated documents that are used to identify amounts owing in regards to the purchase or supply of goods and services. Invoices are formal documents that are used in organisations as a record of how much needs to be paid in or out of the company.

Invoice
S.J Trading

Invoice Number: ST1234/09OP   Customer: J. Spencer

Date: 18 April 2006

Item Number: W167-34   Quantity: 48

Item Description:

4.5" rubber belts (black reinforced)
_____
_____
_____
_____
_____

Unit Price: £0.26   **Amount: £12.48**

Balance to be paid within 30 days of the invoice date:

Figure 1.9

Invoice example

Extended formal document examples

Reports

Reports are used to collect information that can then be distributed to other users. A report can bring together a number of thoughts and ideas that have been investigated and researched. A report may contain a mix of quantitative and qualitative information. The main focus of a report is to deliver any findings in a structured format that ends with a conclusion and possible recommendations on which future action can be taken. An example of a report format can be found in Figure 1.10.

Report template

Title Page:

- front sheet identifying the report title, the author, date and who the report is commissioned for

---

Staff Restructuring Proposals

Author: Jonathon Hayward

22 May 2006
Commissioned for Human Resources

Contents page:

- page referencing the information given on each page, should follow the title page.

Contents

1.0 Introduction

The introduction should provide a short summary of the overall focus and content of the report

2.0 Procedures

Identification of any procedures used to collect, collate, analyse and present information

Figure 1.10

Sample report format

3.0 Main findings

The main findings section is where the bulk of the report content should be placed. The main findings section should be broken down into task, action or research areas. Each area of the findings section should put forward arguments or statements supported by research and analysis. The main findings section can be broken down into sub-sections, for example:

3.1 Marketing resources

3.1.1 New website design
3.1.2 Marketing budget for 2006/7

3.2 Finance resources
3.3 Staff Training

4.0 Conclusions

The conclusion section brings together all of the items discussed within the main findings section and provide a summary of the key areas identified.

5.0 Recommendations

This section is solution based, providing the subjects of the report with proposals as to how they can move forward with the report objective. For example recommendations for staff training could include:

1 Provide management training to all supervisors and section managers
2 Offer in-house ICT training programmes to all data entry clerks within the marketing department
3 Set up staff training services on a rotary basis of three employees each week for eight weeks

6.0 References

This section should identify and give credit for all information sources used to include; books, magazines, journals, reports, and the Internet etc.

Appendix

This section will provide supporting documentation to give additionality to the report content. Appendices could include lists of facts and figures, leaflets, downloaded information, photocopied material etc.

Figure 1.10

continued

What does this mean?

Quantitative information

Quantitative information is based on facts and statistics, key information used for finance, planning and modelling, etc. Examples of this type of information include sales figures, control measurements and test data for an experiment. There is a great need for information of this type if you work within mathematical, science, medical or logic-orientated-type environments where calculations and experimentation plays a dominant role in day-to-day tasks.

Qualitative information

Qualitative information provides the depth and detail to information. The qualitative aspect gives an insight into a subject matter at a much greater level than quantitative information provides.

The basis of qualitative information is to probe and question in order to gain an understanding of the subject matter, for example, students studying for a BTEC First qualification. Statistics might have been generated to identify retention and achievement rates as a percentage based on similar conditions across the country. However the qualitative aspect might illustrate through the use of a course feedback form, which modules students enjoyed, how they felt about assessments, support and resource issues that may have helped them to achieve, etc.

The best ways to extract qualitative information is through interviewing, questionnaires, feedback forms and surveys.

Activity 1

(a) Design a questionnaire to satisfy one of the following:
  (i) Survey types and frequency of magazine purchases
  (ii) Investigate the best film of the year.
  For each questionnaire include a mixture of fifteen qualitative and quantitative questions. When the design is complete, print off or e-mail ten copies to people within the group and get them to complete it

(b) Provide a short summary that identifies which was the easier of the two sets of information, qualitative or quantitative to produce. Why do you think this is?

Graphical document examples

Illustrations

Illustrations can be used for many different purposes. Ultimately they are used to display information and possibly inform a particular audience, such as a map, diagram of the human body or a plan for a new housing development as shown in Figure 1.11.

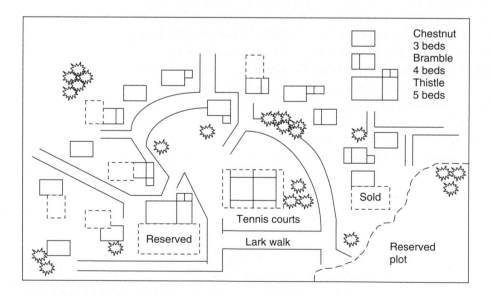

Figure 1.11
Housing development illustration

Information flow diagrams are another example of how information can be displayed more appropriately and effectively in a visual format. Information flows can show how information is exchanged within an organisation and how an organisation interacts with third parties outside of an organisation.

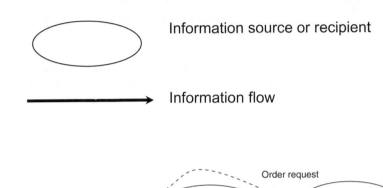

Information source or recipient

Information flow

Figure 1.12

Information flow diagram components

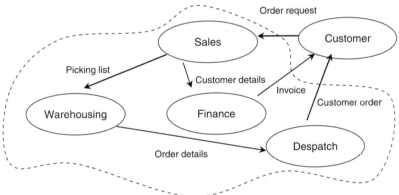

Figure 1.13

Information flow diagram

Promotional document examples

There are a number of documents that can be used to promote a particular product or service. Organisations of all shapes and sizes use a range of advertisement mediums such as leaflets, company information packs and company websites, etc. to create public awareness.

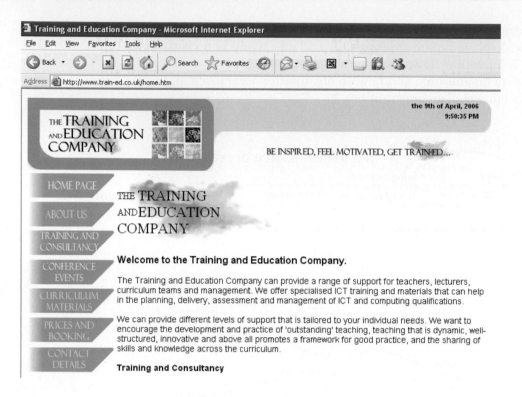

Figure 1.14

Sample website

Informal documents

Informal documents are becoming more and more popular with both the younger and older generation. For the younger generation the growing popularity of mobile phone technology and the use of 'text messaging' or 'texting' has created a new communication language based on abbreviations and smilies as shown in Figure 1.15.

Abbreviations:

M8	Mate
GR8	Great
ATB	All the best
BTW	By the way
CID	Consider it done
CUL8R	See you later
EZ	Easy
H&K	Hug and kiss
LOL	Laughed out loud / Lot's of luck

Smilies

:-)	Happy
:-D	Grinning
:-7	Smirk
:-x	Small kiss
:-X	Big sloppy kiss
<3	A love heart
@--^----	A rose
:'-(	Crying
%-(	Confused and unhappy

Figure 1.15

Examples of abbreviations and smilies in text messaging

Activity 2

(a) Can you add to either of the lists with additional abbreviations and/or smilies

(b) Compose a text message using at least five abbreviations and three smilies.

For the older generation the ability to access information, be sent alerts and updates via text such as timetable information and booking codes has contributed to increase in this informal way of communicating.

What is appropriate communication?

Using a particular document to convey information is only one of many ways of communicating. Communication can be delivered in a range of other formats and the appropriateness of each format can depend upon a number of factors as shown in Figure 1.16. In addition, appropriate communication can also be defined by how it meets user needs and the success of information delivery.

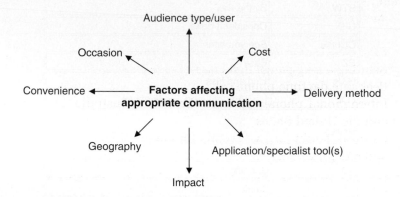

Figure 1.16

Factors affecting appropriate communication

Audience type/user

Your audience, or the person that you are trying to deliver information to, will have an impact upon how information is delivered and the appropriateness of the information. Within an organisation you might chat informally to a colleague, e-mail a team leader and send a memorandum to the department. Socially you might decide to text or send an 'msn' to a friend to arrange a night out.

In terms of appropriate communication when you are trying to relay information to an individual(s) you must also ensure that an appropriate language is used in terms of terminology, level, clarity and writing style.

Cost

The cost of communicating can have an impact on 'appropriateness'. For example, the least expensive way of sending information may also be the least appropriate – sending an e-mail to inform somebody that they have got the job they applied for. Alternatively the most expensive way of sending information may be the most appropriate.

Activity 3

Identify the cost of the following communication services and give an example of the type of message/information that could be sent using this method.

- First class stamp
- Sending a 1-kg parcel first class
- Peak rate daytime phone call
- International phone call from the UK to Australia, Hong Kong and the United States
- Off-peak tariffs for two mobile phone providers (one for texting and one for calls).

Delivery method

Information can be delivered in a number of different ways that can be categorised under the headings of:

(1) Verbal communication
(2) Written communication
(3) Visual communication
(4) Expressive communication

Verbal communication   Verbal communication implies that information has been transmitted through speech. Categories of verbal communication can include:

- Chatting
- Enquiring
- Apologising
- Delegating
- Directing
- Advising
- Informing
- Challenging
- Debating
- Persuading

Activity 4

(a) For each of the verbal categories of communication identify a situation that you have been in which reflects this category

(b) Choose five categories and identify how you influenced the situation through this category of verbal communication

(c) Identify another appropriate category of verbal communication that could have been used instead

(d) Are there any other categories of verbal communication that you can add to the list?

(e) For each of the following scenarios identify the most appropriate verbal communication category and state why, use a table template to complete the information.

Scenario	Verbal communication used	Why?
• Attending an interview		
• Buying a new computer game in a shop		
• You have forgotten your friend's birthday		
• Asking your parents to lend you some money		
• Giving a presentation in 'Using ICT to present information'		

Speaking to somebody face-to-face is one of the most open forms of communication and sometimes the most appropriate. Speech can be spontaneous, emotional, very impressionable and also very personal in some instances.

People communicate with each other every second every day all over the world and for each conversation a unique bond can form between the sender and the receiver. This bond could last a moment or a lifetime. People always say that first impressions count and this is very true. From the moment that you open your mouth to welcome, enquire, dispute or inform, people lock on to what you are saying and react – appropriately or in some cases inappropriately.

Activity 5

(a) Think of a situation where you have been angry and have argued or said things that you didn't mean

(b) What triggered the argument?

(c) What could you have done or said to stop the argument from taking place?

(d) What could you have said during the argument to have made the situation better?

Advantages of verbal communication

Verbal communication has its advantages in that it can be a very open format of communication especially if it is face-to-face. Other advantages can cover areas such as:

• Directed to a specific and the correct audience
• Can generate an instant response or action
• Can complete the communication cycle of controlling a situation and also providing feedback
• Address a single or a multiple audience
• Very expressive
• Inexpensive or free.

Disadvantages of verbal communication

One of the major disadvantages of verbal communication is the fact that it is all too easy to say things in the spare of the moment. These things may not have been said if another form of communication had been used. It is easier to express anger verbally than it is to write it down in a letter. The disadvantage being the spontaneity of verbal communication, and the lack of control over emotions, that can then spill into conversations or disputes.

Written communication Written documents can vary in terms of style and layout as discussed in Section 'Short formal document formats'. They can also be classified more broadly in terms of being *formal* and *informal*. Formal written communication relates to official documents which provide guarantees and assurances, these documents can be legally binding. Informal written communication can include a letter to a friend, memos, e-mails and greetings, etc.

Activity 6

For each of the following written documents, identify those that fall into a formal category and those that can be considered as informal.

Letter to a friend	Birth certificate	Receipt
Application form	Statement for a phone bill	Birthday card
Contract of employment	Booking confirmation for a holiday	
Driving licence Curriculum vitae	E-mail to a colleague	Memo
Agenda for a meeting	Newspaper	Letter of resignation

Written communication is of great importance because of the warranty or assurances that it provides. Filling in an application form, for example, is identifying and providing assurances of the knowledge and skills of the applicant. Producing a curriculum vitae (CV) provides a written confirmation of ability and suitability for a particular task. A receipt is a warranty verifying the sale of an item. Certificates verify an achievement in a particular area such as swimming, qualifications or marriage. Birthday cards provide an acknowledgement of a celebration.

Written communication can take on a number of forms and serve a range of purposes and audiences. Over recent years written communication has become even more popular due to the increasing interest of electronic mail (e-mail) and text messaging. These methods provide the flexibility and convenience which traditional letter writing lacks. With an e-mail or text, information can be sent immediately and with less expense than traditional postage methods. Responses are faster, in some cases instant, with no restriction on postage times. The result, written communication has again become fashionable, especially amongst the younger generation with the added bonus of convenience, flexibility and its ability to be interactive.

Visual communication   Visual communication incorporates a range of pictorial, graphical, design and interactive tools that can be more appropriate than other forms of communication.

Visual communication is an integral part of everyday life, examples can be found wherever we go.

Examples of visual communication include: maps, pictures, graphs, static and moving images, charts, draft designs and drawings, etc.

Activity 7

To emphasise the importance of visual communication, carry out the following exercise in groups of three.

(a) One person within the group should draw up a set of written instructions of how to get from one familiar location to another, A–B

(b) In collaboration with the second team member, the instructions should be read out, to enable them to draw a map of how to get from A to B

(c) Together both team members should then present the two formats of instructions to the third team member so that they can identify which of the two formats is more appropriate and clearer to understand, giving reasons.

Expressive communication Finally communicating information expressively through the use of body language, sign language and gestures is indeed very appropriate in certain situations, for example, a handshake to welcome a delegate to a meeting.

a   e   i   p   y

Figure 1.17

Examples of expressive communication – sign language

Expressive communication can include a range of actions such as:

• Smiling
• Frowning
• Hugging
• Waving
• Laughing
• Crying
• Kissing

Each action communicates a specific thought or mood, for example, you might frown to express your discontent at a situation or smile to welcome or express happiness.

Discontented

Surprised

Happy

Angry

Secretive

Figure 1.18

Examples of facial expressive communication

Activity 8

(a)   Identify all the different body language actions that you used yesterday and identify where, when and to whom you expressed these

(b)   Would it have been more appropriate to have used an alternative expressive action, and if so, which?

(c)   Within small groups discuss different formats of information and from the discussion produce a table similar to the one provided identifying three identifying three categories with an example for each format.

For example 'giving advice' would be a suitable verbal format of information, the example being 'providing a recommendation to a friend that wants to buy a PC'.

Category	Format	Example
Verbal	1. Giving advice	Providing a recommendation to a friend that wants to buy a PC
	2.	
	3.	
Written	1.	
	2.	
	3.	
Visual	1.	
	2.	
	3.	
Expressive	1.	
	2.	
	3.	

Application/specialist tools

The appropriateness of communication can be influenced by the use of application packages and specialist tools. Application packages such as word processors, spreadsheets, databases, desk-top publishing, graphics and communication packages can enhance the way in which information is communicated. The use of processing, manipulation and editing tools can ensure that information is displayed correctly, checked grammatically, sorted accordingly and displayed visually in an easy and user-friendly format.

In terms of specialist tools, functions and options such as readability tests, netiquette, summaries and templates can also provide the user with a package of knowledge and skills that will enable them to design and create information documents in an information documenn appropriate format.

What does this mean?

Netiquette: standard conventions that set out guidelines for communicating on electronic forums/message boards, mail groups and newsgroups. It specifies the 'do's' and 'don'ts' of interacting and posting messages.

Impact

When discussing the appropriateness of communication, this can be linked strongly to the type of impression or impact that you want to create. You would not finalise a new finance strategy for your organisation with your bank by sending an e-mail, you might deliver a presentation, set up a meeting or send in a written proposal.

Geography

The distance over which communication has to travel can determine the type and appropriateness of the delivery tool to be used. It would not be feasible to shout over a distance of ten miles, it would be more practical to use the telephone, send a text message or an e-mail.

Convenience

Appropriate communication can be influenced by how quickly, how cheaply, how far or how convenient it is to use a particular method. Convenience may determine that although you would like to sit down and write a letter to a friend, because of a range of other factors it would be more convenient to pick up the telephone or send an e-mail.

Test your knowledge

There are a number of factors that can impact upon appropriate communication. Identify six of these factors and give an example of each.

Software that can be used for presenting and communicating information

Information can be presented in a variety of formats as previously explored. However, there are a number of factors that can enhance the way in which we present and communicate information, one of these being the use of 'appropriate software'.

Software can be categorised into a number of different groups that determine the role and function of what the software can do, examples of these include:

- Application software
- Operating system software
- Utility software
- Communications software

In terms of presenting and communicating information this would fall under the role of applications software – software that we use to create, edit and present information.

Applications software

There are a number of different types of application software, which range from text-based software that can be used to create documents such as letters, memos and reports.

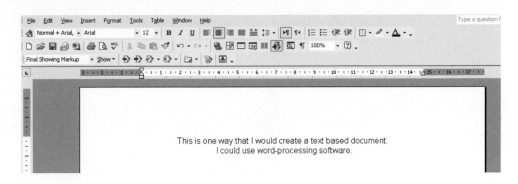

Figure 1.19

Text-based example – text editors and word processors

Other types of software include graphics software that can be used to enhance documents and create visual documents such as menus, newsletters, posters, leaflets and invitations. Graphics can also be used to generate logos and letterheads.

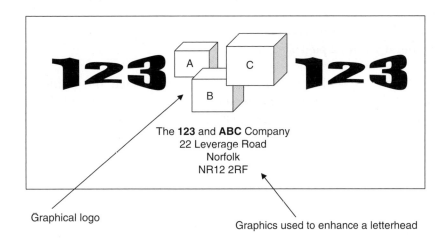

Figure 1.20

Example of a graphical logo

Graphics software and tools can be found within a package or as a stand-alone graphics package.

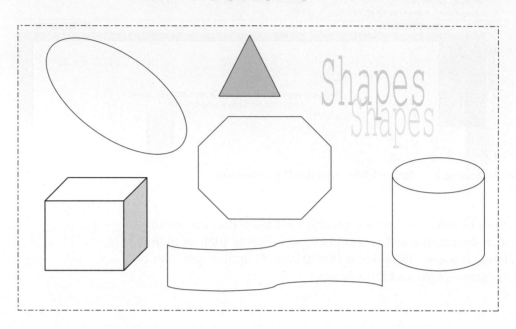

Figure 1.21

Graphical tools found within a package

Within a stand-alone graphics package, the graphical tools are more advanced with better options, colours and editing features. Stand-alone graphics packages can be used to create a range of professional documents such as marketing and promotional materials for organisations.

Figure 1.22

Features of a stand-alone graphics package

Presentation software

Presentation software can be used to graphically and interactively present information. Within a slide presentation sequences of screens can be put together to include text, graphics and different page lay-outs. In addition, multimedia sound and moving images can also be inserted to make the presentation style more dynamic.

ICT has played a big role in the way in which presentations are delivered and the overall quality of presentations. Software applications can be used for the specific purpose of delivering a professional presentation. Presentation software today can provide a number of benefits.

Benefits of using presentation software

- Can be quick and easy to use
- Provides step-by-step designs
- Allows for interactivity
- Incorporates sound and images both static and moving
- Widely available
- Customise each presentation.

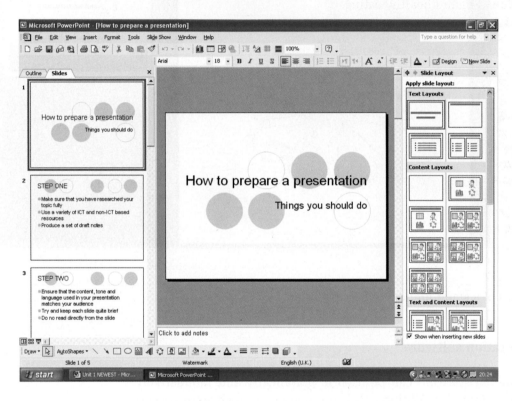

Figure 1.23

Example of presentation software

Presentation software can provide a whole range of features that will enable you to:

- Customise slide background/wallpaper
- Control the speed of each slide
- Determine the way in which the slide appears onto the screen (e.g. dissolving in)
- Automatically time the length of each slide
- Link to other applications or the Web.

Activity 9

Prepare a five-minute presentation to include up to 10 slides on one of the following subjects:

(a)   A sporting activity or event
(b)   Planning a holiday
(c)   A film or book review
(d)   Nutrition and healthy eating.

Apart from applications software, there are a range of other technologies that can be used for presenting and communicating information, such as texting on mobile phones or sending a multimedia file, sending an e-mail, using a webcam or video phone.

Information can be presented in a variety of formats using a range of applications. The way in which we access information, input, process and output information can vary greatly between systems, hardware, software and end user. In terms of the actual interface there are a variety of ways that a user can physically communicate or interact with a system. This can include the use of touch screens and pads to select options from a menu system, the use of a WIMP (Windows, Icons, Mouse, Pointer) interface such as the 'Windows' environment used on a wide range of PC-based systems. A GUI (Graphical User Interface) system is also available in a wide range of systems such as mobile phones, games consoles, cash dispensers and satellite navigation systems. In some environments certain tasks such as installations, upgrades and scripting may require an interface that is 'command based' as oppose to 'point and click'.

Information can be captured using a variety of both ICT- and non-ICT-based resources, and once captured it can be output in a number of different formats as shown in Figure 1.24.

Key point

ICT-based resources can include information from the Internet, attachments sent in an e-mail, specialist CD-ROMs such as articles from newspapers, electronic magazines and journals. Non-ICT-based resources can include information gathered from a third party, for example, a teacher/lecturer, employer or friend, books or magazines, etc.

Key point

Whenever information is exchanged it should be checked to make sure that it is valid. The validity of information is important if you are going to pass it onto a third party or use it in a document or presentation. Checking the validity of information could involve checking the source of the information for accuracy or checking the currency of information to see how up-to-date it is.

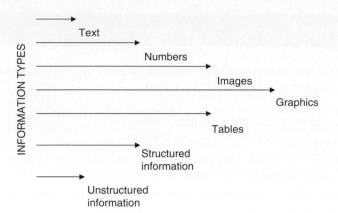

Figure 1.24

Information types

Each format is quite unique in that it has its own set of qualities in terms of audience appropriateness, awareness and impact, formality and occasion as previously discussed.

Commonly used tools and techniques in application packages

Software application packages are designed to support users in the creation, editing and updating of information. Although the large majority of applications packages appear to be quite standard in terms of layout, the tools and techniques available provide the user with an opportunity to transform a standard document into a customised, individual creation.

It is essential that information is presented clearly. Good presentation skills and the use of presentation techniques are essential in all environments; people will have expectations on your ability to present information clearly, cohesively, relevantly and knowledgeably. In conjunction, the ability to format and edit documents is also important from a user's perspective because they can take control and customise the layout of a document to meet a given requirement.

The way in which a message, thought or idea is presented can have a strong impact upon the recipient of that message. To help understand the different styles and presentation of information, this section will introduce you to a range of tools and techniques that will allow you to format, edit and present different documents.

There are a number of ways that text can be formatted and edited in terms of:

- Individual characters
- Paragraphs
- Pages

You can change the way a single character looks by using a different colour, font or size (as shown in the next section). You can change a paragraph by inserting or deleting text, indenting sections or use a variety of features such as bulleting or numbering to make sections of text stand out. A page can be edited/formatted by changing its appearance in terms of inserting a graphic, copying and pasting information, adding a border, changing its orientation – from portrait to landscape or through the use of advanced tools. All of these features can be used to enhance the page using a combination of text, graphics, paragraph styles and tracking tools.

In terms of using graphics, tools can also be used to change quite a basic graphic into a sophisticated and individual design by using a variety of image features such as shape rotation and flip and drawing features to include lines, shapes, paint and airbrush facilities.

Page layout features

There are a number of ways that you can customise your page layout to incorporate a number of features, some of these can include:

- setting the margins to inset certain information and emphasise certain sections of text
- using headers and footers to enclose information such as the document name, date created, author and page number
- orientating the page to change between portrait and landscape
- changing the paper size from A4 to A3, for example.

Setting the margins

Margins can be set left, right, top or bottom to leave a gap before the text or graphics start on a document. Margins may need to be set up to fit in around pre-printed headers, footers or side logos. Margins may also be set to leave an edge all around the document to improve its appearance or to make it easier to read.

Formatting and editing features commonly used in text-based documents

By using the margin feature text can be inset top, bottom left and right

Figure 1.25

How to set up margins

Headers and footers

Headers and footers can help to enhance the style and formality of a document, they should provide meaningful information about the author of the document, the date of creation, filename and page numbers, etc.

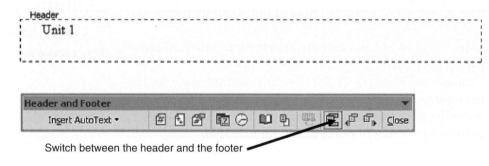

Switch between the header and the footer

Figure 1.26

Example of a header

Page orientation

The way in which a page is set-out can have a dramatic impact on how the information will be received by an intended audience. For example, in terms of orientation will the page be 'portrait' or 'landscape'.

Figure 1.27

Page orientation

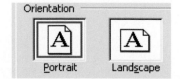

Documents such as letters, reports and most business documents are 'portrait' style. Other considerations might include – how the information is going to be set-out on the page – in column format, frames, text, insertion of graphics, tables, charts, etc.

Paper size

Paper size will vary depending upon the type of document being created, for example, A2, A3, A4 or A5. The relationship between paper sizes is that A3 is double the size of A4, A4 is double the size of A5, etc. Most standard documents such as letters and reports are A4, although you need to ensure that the letter size is set for UK and not US standards. User guides and newsletters however may use smaller or larger paper sizes to emphasise or consolidate the information.

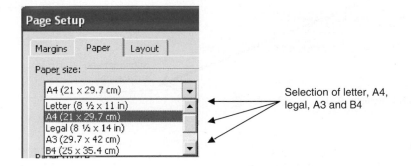

Selection of letter, A4, legal, A3 and B4

Figure 1.28
Changing the page size

Changing the font format and style

In order to make a document look more professional and creative a range of text and presentation styles can also be included. In terms of text styles, consideration has to be made as to what font is going to be used, what style or size or format – bold, italic, underline, superscript or subscript.

- Changing **of** fo*nts*
- Heading and title styles
- **Using bold**, *italic* and <u>underline</u>
- Superscript and subscript

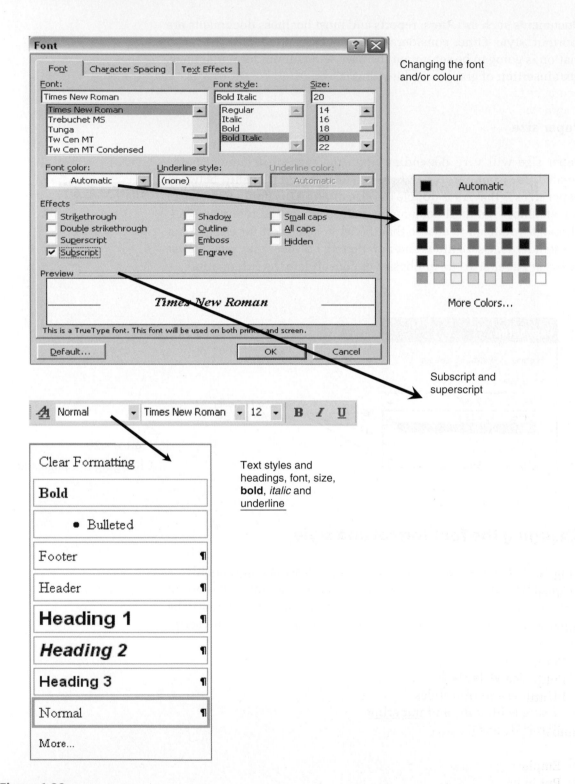

Changing the font and/or colour

Subscript and superscript

Text styles and headings, font, size, **bold**, *italic* and underline

Figure 1.29
Examples of font format and style

Presentation styles can be created by using tabs and indents, paragraph numbering, bullet points and hyphenation.

Tabs and indents will enable you to set up pre-defined sections in any document that you are working on. In conjunction indents for new paragraphs, etc. can be defined to enhance the style of the document.

Tabs   Indents

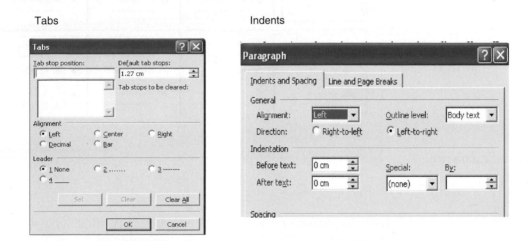

Figure 1.30
Tabs and indents

Paragraph numbering is very useful in certain documents such as reports where automatic numbering can be used to section out areas of the report. Paragraph numbering – for example, in a report can be done manually, or once the report is complete it can be applied to the finished document.

Bullets and numbering can be used to emphasise certain parts of a document in a list format, for example:

Bullets can be used to

- Emphasise certain text
- Put information into an orderly list
- Identify key features within certain information.

Numbering would have the same effect:

(1) Emphasise certain text
(2) Put information into an orderly list
(3) Identify key features within certain information.

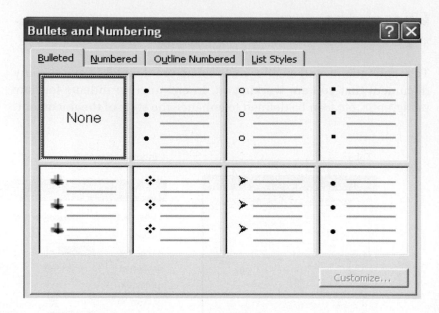

Figure 1.31

Bullets and numbering

With hyphenation, Word will automatically fit a long word that appears at the end of a line to the beginning of a new line instead of hyphenating it. Hyphenation can also be used to insert hyphens, when needed within a document.

Activity 10

Create a menu for a restaurant that consists of three courses:

- A starter
- Main course
- Dessert

The menu should include a range of the following features: different fonts and sizes, indented or bulleted information and an appropriate header or footer.

Lines and borders

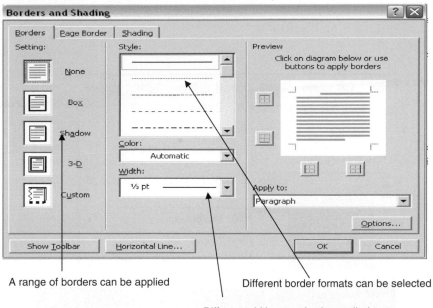

A range of borders can be applied

Different border formats can be selected

Different widths can also be applied

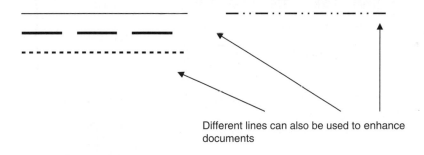

Different lines can also be used to enhance documents

Figure 1.32

Lines and borders

Creating columns and tables

Columns can be used to divide the page into appropriate sections that will allow you to set up templates for documents such as newsletters and leaflets.

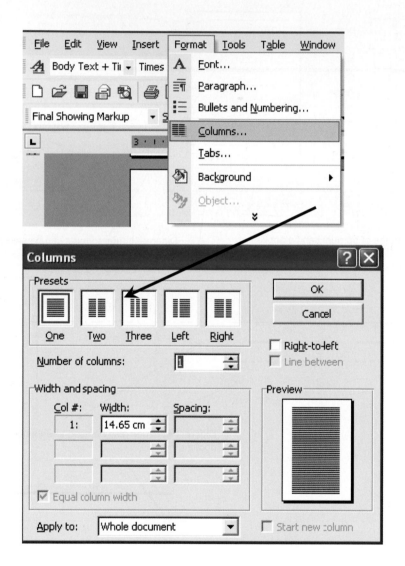

Figure 1.33

Setting up a column

Activity 11

Set up a one-page A4 portrait newsletter using at least a two-column format. The newsletter should be based on one of the following topics:

(i)   A recent film or book review
(ii) A sporting event
(iii) A report on a current media event.

Tables

Tables are used for a variety of contexts and they are very easy to set up and modify.

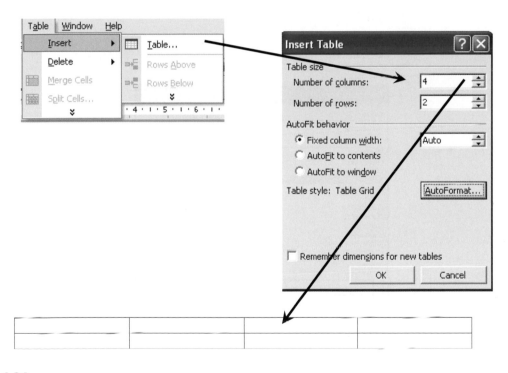

Figure 1.34
Setting up a table

Once a table has been set up – as shown in Figure 1.34, it can also be modified very easily by using 'autoformat' features.

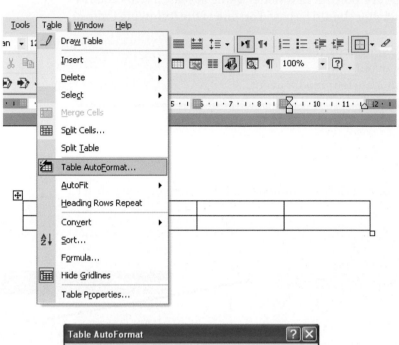

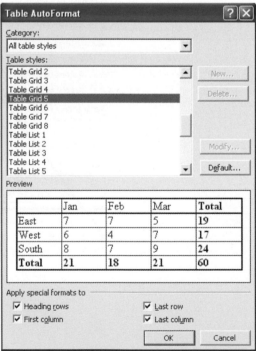

Figure 1.35

Using table autoformat features

Graphs and charts

Graphs and charts will provide a more visual overview of any data that you have generated in your spreadsheet. There are a number of graphs and charts that can be used. Some of these include

- Pie charts
- Bar graphs
- Line graphs
- Scatter graphs

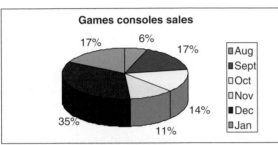

Pie charts

Each segment of the pie chart represents a percentage of games consoles sold for each month from August to January. The smallest segment is 6% for August and the largest is 35% for December.

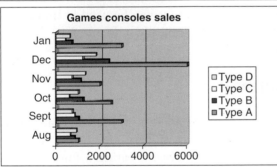

Bar graphs

The bars on the graph each represent a type of games console ranging from A to D. The bar graph identifies for each month, how many of each console was sold.

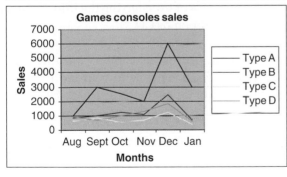

Line graph

The line graph clearly plots the sales of each console from August to January. It is very evident that Type A console is the best seller and Type C console is the worst seller. From this graph it is also clear that in August, September and January sales were very similar for Types B, C and D.

Figure 1.36
Examples of charts and graphs

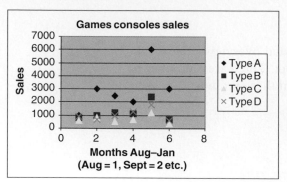

Scatter graph

Scatter graphs are best used when there is a lot of numerical data that requires plotting to identify a correlation or pattern in the data. This specific scatter graph shows the pattern of sales for each month 1–6. In August it clearly shows that all four games console types had similar sales figures, however in December these are quite diverse.

Figure 1.36
Continued

There are a wide range of presentation techniques available to enhance both text and graphical documents. Some of these techniques range from a basic level that includes changing the style, colour or layout of text, through to the use of columns, tables, headers and footers, bullets and the integration of graphics. At the other end of the scale advanced techniques can be used to include a table of contents, indexes and speaker notes to a document.

Storage of information

Once a document has been created it is important that it is stored safely for future reference. Information storage could simply mean saving a document in a specific area, creating a folder and saving information to that particular area or transferring the information onto another medium such as a USB pen or CD.

Saving a file is quite a simple process as shown and unless the file doesn't become corrupt, or there is damage to your hard disk is usually quite a permanent method of is usually quite a permanent method of storage.

Saving a file

Click on 'File' – 'Save As' and a dialogue box will appear prompting the user to provide a file name and location to save to.

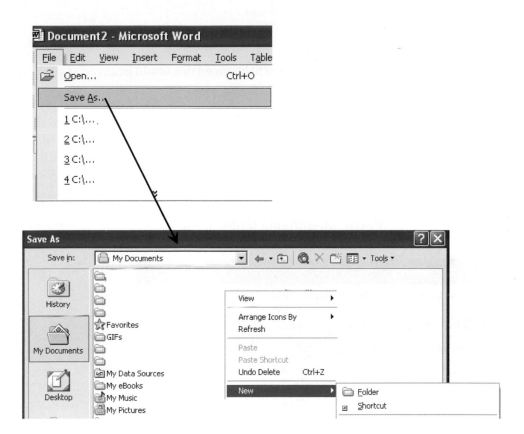

Figure 1.37
Saving files

By right-clicking in the 'Save As' dialogue box the user then has the option to create a new folder to store a document in. For example, a folder titled 'assignments' may have documents saved for each unit of study.

Depending upon the type of file being saved you may have to select a specific format.

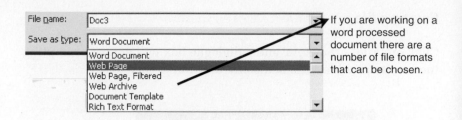

If you are working on a word processed document there are a number of file formats that can be chosen.

Figure 1.38

Saving files in a particular format

If a graphics file was to be saved this could be saved as a 'bitmap' .bmp, gif or tiff format, for example.

Once documents have been saved you need to ensure that you can find them easily. By applying good file management skills such as meaningful names and ensuring that files and folders are kept updated and orderly there should be no issues regarding 'lost' files.

Easily identifiable folder names

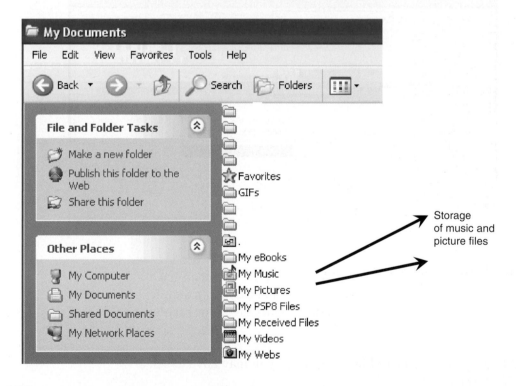

Storage of music and picture files

Figure 1.39

Labelling files for easy identification

Once folders have been set up, they can easily be edited, moved or deleted making file management more efficient.

Creating shortcuts and renaming folders

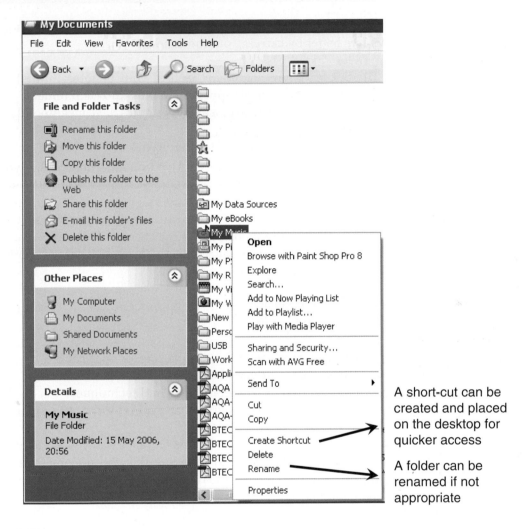

A short-cut can be created and placed on the desktop for quicker access

A folder can be renamed if not appropriate

Figure 1.40
Creating shortcuts and renaming folders

Activity 12

Based on the information provided, start to organise your files and folders better by carrying out the following tasks:

(i)   Set up a new folder for each of your chapters (units) on the course and transfer appropriate files into each folder
(ii) Check to make sure that all of your files have meaningful names, if not, rename them
(iii) Check that any other files that have not been placed in a folder can be found easily.

Reviewing and adjusting documents

Once a document is complete there are a number of things that should be checked prior to submission. These checks can be carried out manually by the user and also electronically through the use of application tools.

Following this review and checking process it is also good practice to evaluate and justify:

- why you have used a certain package or application?
- why you have designed a document in a particular way?
- why you have used certain tools and techniques?
- why you have used a particular layout, format or template?

Once this evaluative process has taken place and you are happy with the final document you can then say that the document is 'fit for purpose' and that it meets the requirements and needs of a particular target audience(s).

Managing your work

When managing your work you should consider a number of issues that may affect the quality, accuracy and security of anything that you produce.

In terms of good practice you could draw up a plan of activities that you intend to undertake throughout any work or project that you are doing. This plan could include interim dates for hand-in, such as the example provided.

Work plan				
Tasks to complete	**Resources required (books, etc.)**	**Date to be submitted**	**Deadline met**	**Problems/issues encountered**
1				
2				
3				
4				

When work is submitted, you should ensure that each page has a header and a footer, in which your name is clearly identified.

Activity 13

Based on the template provided try and create your own version of a work plan. You might want to consider adding in more information, such as:

(i) Application used
(ii) Details of where the file has been saved to
(iii) A checklist of considerations that can be ticked off when completed (as shown below).

When submitting your work, also ensure that you have kept evidence of previous versions and drafts produced. When your work is saved you should try and keep it in an orderly format using good file structure so that files can be easily recognised.

Other areas to consider before handing in any work include:

✓ Has the document been proofread and grammar checked?
✓ Has the document been spell-checked?
✓ Is the document in the correct layout?
✓ Is the document appropriate for the target audience?
✓ Does the document meet the requirements of the brief/task/ assignment?

Chapter 2

Introduction to computer systems

This unit will enable students to gain an insight into computer systems in terms of different types of components, hardware and software that make up a computer. Students will appreciate the difference between different types of software and their function, for example, applications software, utility and operating systems software.

Students will be involved in a number of practical elements within this unit and will demonstrate how various devices can be connected and software configured.

This unit will allow students to make informed choices about computing requirements for different types of end user, for example, business use and home use and facilitate them in making judgements about the needs of different users in terms of both hardware and software.

Throughout this unit you will also be introduced to a range of issues concerning computer security, health and safety and legislation that protects the rights of users of computers in terms of Data Protection Act 1988 and Computer Misuse Act 1990.

When you complete this unit you should be able to:

(1) Know different uses of computers in homes and businesses
(2) Be able to explain the use of common types of hardware in a personal computer system
(3) Know how to select software for a specified user
(4) Be able to safely connect hardware devices and configure software for a specified user.

Uses of a computer

Computer technology now appears in almost everything, their sophisticated processing and management system guiding us through almost every aspect of our lives.

On that basis we use computers in our phones, cars, washing machines and even in fridges. Computers help us to communicate, navigate, keep clean and keep cool. Gone are the days when computers were confined to huge rooms with buttons, wheels and reels. Welcome to the 21st century, where small is beautiful.

A computer can be defined as any number of the following,

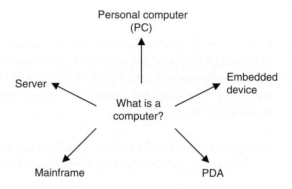

Figure 2.1

What defines a computer?

Personal computer

PCs seem to be quite a common feature in most households and a necessity for most businesses. With prices starting from under £300, the growth and popularity of home computing has grown over the past 5 years. A computer can be defined as any device that will accept and process data and generate a set of results. However personal computers are more recognisable as desktop devices that have a combination of input, output, storage, arithmetic, logic and control units.

Embedded device

From washing machines to satellite navigation, game consoles to mobile phones, computers seem to be embedded in a diverse range of gadgets. Embedded devices have the capability of providing precision directions to a specified location or address. In addition they can provide a fantasy world of interactive gaming with state of the art multimedia functions or the ability to communicate across continents with the touch of a button on a portable, wireless device.

Personal Digital Assistant (PDA)

A handheld device originally used as a personal organiser, however over the years they have grown into a device that has many functions, including the integration of games and applications and the ability to access e-mail and the Internet through Wi-Fi connectivity.

Figure 2.2
PDA

Mainframe

A mainframe is a very large computer that has the capability of supporting multiple users (hundreds or even thousands) at the same time. These are found in organisational environments because of their price.

Server

A computer or device on a network that has the function of providing a service to other resources, for example, a print server, web server, e-mail server or newsgroup server.

Activity 1

(a)   Carry out research to identify at least two specific items that have embedded computer devices

(b)   PDAs are very popular for communicating on the move, in the absence of a desktop or laptop device. Produce a one-page information leaflet on PDAs to include a range of the following items:
  *   Types of PDA
  *   Prices
  *   Features
  *   Benefits
  *   Users

Computer users and usages

The growth in computers has opened up the gateway for a number of different users that may not have thought about interacting with computing technology. Users can be categorised broadly into two areas:

(1)   Home – personal user
(2)   Business – commercial, educational, industrial, financial user.

Within these categories, users can be further divided in terms of their level of expertise, for example, novice, intermediate, advanced and their level of interaction – what tasks they carry out (what they use the computer for).

Home users use computers for a wide range of tasks as shown in Figure 2.3.

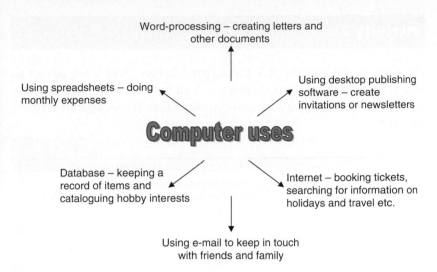

Word-processing – creating letters and other documents

Using desktop publishing software – create invitations or newsletters

Using spreadsheets – doing monthly expenses

Computer uses

Database – keeping a record of items and cataloguing hobby interests

Internet – booking tickets, searching for information on holidays and travel etc.

Using e-mail to keep in touch with friends and family

Figure 2.3

Computer uses

Uses of a computer

Home computing includes children accessing information for educational purposes, parents accessing information for recreational purposes, users working from home, retired people 'silver surfers' that use computers for keeping in touch via e-mail, the Internet and through possible on-line clubs and societies.

The use of computers in business ranges widely because of the various sectors of industry.

Sectors of industry include:

- Finance
- Education and Training
- Medicine
- Retail
- Manufacturing
- Government
- Military
- Charity
- Agriculture
- Technology
- Logistics

Within these sectors, there will be computer users working at a number of levels. Some users will include data processing clerks, word-processing/administration personnel, end user support/help desk, web designers, programmers, technical support/technicians.

Activity 2

For each of the specific ICT tasks listed below, find a job advert to match three of the task requirements. You may decide to find a single advert that covers at least three requirements or three separate adverts for each.

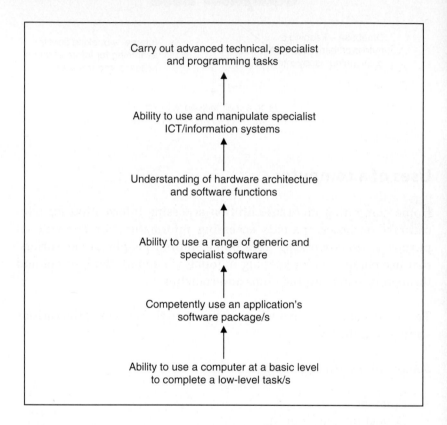

Whether be it a home or business user, computers will always be used for a variety of tasks, and because of this there will always be different levels of users from the novice that uses a computer for the occasional letter writing to the more intermediate that uses a range of software to carry out a specific job, role or task. Finally at a more advanced level there will always be a need for technical expertise, users to write programs, design websites and configure hardware and software.

User interfaces

A number of different user interfaces exist, some of these are graphical such as Microsoft Windows and some are text or command based such as MS-DOS and Linux.

User interfaces are accessed via an input device of some description, this can include:

- A keyboard to type in instructions or commands
- A mouse – point and click device to select from a menu or icon
- A microphone – to facilitate speech recognition and voice-activated commands
- A tracker ball – to navigate to a specific interface command
- Specialist devices associated with various technologies or user abilities.

Activity 3

(a) In small groups carry out research on at least two different types of user interface and prepare a short presentation (no more than 15 min) that addresses each of the following criteria:
   - Full description of the user interface device
   - A graphic/s that shows the user interface
   - An evaluation of the user interface in terms of how it looks, how it is accessed, ease of use and features, etc.

(b) Individually provide a short talk on the user interface (is it colour, does it have icons, is it menu driven, etc.) of a mobile phone. If you do not have your own mobile, try and borrow a friend or family member's phone, or ask an assistant in a phone shop if they can show you the interface features of a mobile.

Common types of hardware in a personal computer system

There are a number of hardware components that go together to make a computer system apart from the power supply unit (PSU), keyboard, mouse and monitor. Other components are:

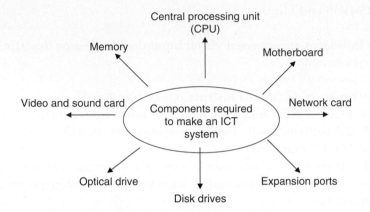

Figure 2.4

Components for a computer system

Central processing unit (CPU)

The CPU is the main chip or processor that connects onto the motherboard in a computer, it is the brain of the computer. The CPU processes data that it fetches or receives from other sources. When people talk about CPUs, in the past they would refer to the clock speed such as 3.2 GHz. With advances in technology however, CPU can be measured against their performance rating. Currently there are two mainstream manufacturers of CPUs that are used in PCs – AMD and Intel.

Motherboard

The motherboard is the main circuit board, that provides the base on which a number of other hardware devices are plugged in. The printed circuits on a motherboard provide the electrical connections between all of the devices that are plugged into it.

Devices that plug into a motherboard include:

- CPU – central processing unit
- BIOS memory
- RAM

In addition there are a number of slots that can be used for expansion boards and cards to provide the system with extra features.

Expansion cards can be used for modems, graphics cards, TV cards, network cards, sound cards and SCSI cards, etc.

To allow communication between different parts of the computer system, a 'bus' system is required. A bus is a group of parallel wires, along which data can flow. The system bus is made up of a number of such communication channels that connect the processor and other components such as memory, input and output devices together. A computer will normally have several buses that are used for specific purposes.

In addition to these components and devices, other features exist within the main processing unit, one of these being a coprocessor. The function of a coprocessor is to speed up certain types of computatations, for example, a graphics accelerator card will sometimes have its own built in.

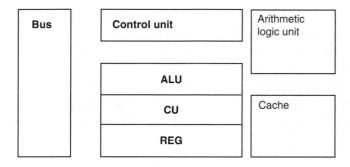

Figure 2.5

Logical representation of a PC system

Network card

A network card – sometimes referred to as a Network Interface Card (NIC). The network card plays a very important role of connecting your cable modem and your computer together. It will enable you to interface with a network through either wires or wireless technologies.

The network card allows data to be transferred from your computer to another computer or device.

Expansion ports

Universal serial bus (USB) provides the connectivity for peripheral devices and in a large majority of current computer systems, supersedes both parallel and serial ports.

A parallel port is an interface for connecting an external device such as a printer to a computer. Most computers have both a parallel port and at least one serial port.

A parallel port uses a 25-pin connector to connect with printers and other devices requiring a relatively high bandwidth.

A serial port is a general-purpose interface that can be used for almost any type of device including modems, mouse and printers (although most printers are connected to a parallel port).

Disk drives and optical drives

Storage devices are essential in a computer system. Storage is required to:

- store programs
- data that is waiting to be processed
- the output of future information.

The need for portable, convenient data storage devices has dictated that technologies become even more dynamic in design and functionality. Over the years, storage devices have changed from tapes to floppy disks, CDs and minidisks to DVDs and USB pens.

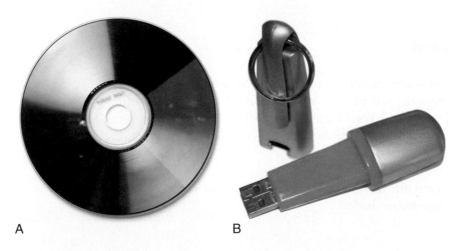

A   B

Figure 2.6

Types of storage devices

Storage requirements differ between user types and organisations. For example, a home user might require 20 gigabytes (Gb) as an entry level for storing data. A small organisation with three or four stand-alone computers might require a minimum of 40 Gb on each. A small networked organisation with up to ten computers running via a server could have anything up to 500 Gb. A large networked organisation running up to fifty computers without individual local drives could require terabyte (Tb) storage.

Disk drives can be either internal or external to a computer; they read data from and write data onto a disk. There are different types of disk drives for different types of disks.

For example, a hard disk drive (HDD) reads and writes hard disks, a floppy disk drive (FDD) accesses floppy disks. A magnetic disk drive reads magnetic disks, and an optical drive reads optical disks.

Video and sound cards

These cards will output video or audio data/information. Without a video card a computer will not function, unless there is an on-board integrated card. A computer will function however without a sound card as computers have integrated speakers although these are very crude in sound output.

Sound cards will enable the computer to output sound through speakers connected to the motherboard to record sound input from a microphone connected to the computer, and manipulate sound stored on a disk.

Nearly all sound cards support MIDI, a standard for representing music electronically. In addition, most sound cards are Sound Blaster-compatible so that they can process commands that have been written for a Sound Blaster card, the de facto standard for PC sound.

Memory

When software is loaded it must be stored somewhere inside the computer. The main storage space for programs inside the computer is called 'memory'. Main memory is divided into a number of cells or locations, each of which has its own unique address.

There are two types of computer memory inside the computer, RAM and ROM.

(1) RAM (random access memory) is the main store. This is the place where programs and software once loaded is stored. When the CPU runs a program, it fetches the program instructions from RAM and executes them.

RAM can have instructions read from it by the CPU and also it can have numbers or other computer data written to it by the CPU. RAM is volatile which means that the main memory can be destroyed, either by being overwritten as new data is entered for processing or when the machine is switched off. Therefore it is not practical to store data files and programs permanently in the main memory.

There are two types of RAM, static and dynamic:

Static RAM (SRAM) is incredibly fast and incredibly expensive, it is used as cache. Cache is a portion of memory made of high-speed static RAM (SRAM) instead of the slower and cheaper dynamic RAM (DRAM) which is used for main memory. Memory caching is effective because most programs access the same data or instructions over and over. By keeping as much of this information as possible in SRAM, the computer avoids accessing the slower DRAM.

DRAM – Dynamic Random Access Memory is used in most personal computers. DRAM chips are available in several forms, the most popular forms are:

- DIP (dual in-line package) that can be soldered directly onto the surface of the circuit board although a socket package can be used in place of soldering
- SOJ (small outline J-lead) and TSOP (thin, small outline package) which can be mounted directly onto the surface of the circuit board.

The more memory (RAM) a computer has, the better it works. To measure how much a computer's memory will store, think of memory as a series of little boxes, referred to as memory locations, each location is able to store a piece of computer data. The more locations that a computer's memory has, provides the key to its overall size. Computer memory is measured in units of 'thousands of locations' and in units of 'millions of locations'.

There are temporary storage areas, built-in RAM known as buffers; they act as a holding area, enabling the CPU to manipulate data before transferring it to a device.

(2)   ROM (read only memory) will allow the CPU to fetch or read instructions from it, however, ROM comes with instructions that are permanently stored inside it and these cannot be overwritten by the computer's CPU. ROM memory is used for storing special sets of instructions which the computer needs when it starts up. When a computer is switched off, the contents of ROM are not erased.

Bit	Smallest unit of measurement	Single binary digit 0 or 1
Byte	Made up of 8 bits, amount of space required to hold a single character	Value between 0 and 255
Kilobyte (Kb)	Equivalent to 1,000 characters	Approximately 1,000 bytes
Megabyte (Mb)	Equivalent to 1 million characters	Approximately 1,000 kilobytes
Gigabyte (Gb)	Equivalent to 1 billion characters	Approximately 1,000 megabytes
Terabyte (Tb)	Equivalent to 1 thousand billion characters	Approximately 1,000 Gigabytes

More recently huge storage capacities have become available to include:

Petabyte	10^{15} 1 000 000 000 000 000	Approximately 1,000 terabytes
Exabyte	10^{18} 1 000 000 000 000 000 000	Approximately 1,000 petabytes
Zettabyte	10^{21} 1 000 000 000 000 000 000 000	Approximately 1,000 exabytes
Yottabyte	10^{24} 1 000 000 000 000 000 000 000 000	Approximately 1,000 zettabytes

Figure 2.7
Memory sizes

To further enhance a computer system a number of other components can be added to provide Internet connection, printing and scanning facilities, video capture, etc.

Test your knowledge

(1) There are a number of components that go to make up a computer system – what are they?
(2) What types of memory are there?
(3) What is the difference(s) between a disk drive and a USB – why might you need a USB pen?
(4) What is the function of the motherboard?
(5) In terms of data representation and memory size place the following units in order of size from the largest to the smallest:
   - Terabyte
   - Zettabyte
   - Kilobyte
   - Bit
   - Gigabyte

Activity 4

There are a number of different components that make up a computer system.

(a) Collect information on three different priced PC's that show a breakdown of their specification (this information can be gathered from newspapers, computer magazines or off the Internet)
(b) For each specification provide a review of the PC, based on certain features such as speed, memory capacity or storage
(c) If you wanted to purchase a PC what features would you look for, and state whether or not any of the three specifications that you have would meet your requirements.

Software

There are a number of different types of software. Some software is designed to support and enable the user to operate the system – operating system software. Other software provides the programs and tools to design, model, input, manipulate and output data. This type of software includes spreadsheets, word processing, databases, graphics, presentation, communication and desktop publishing. This software is referred to as 'applications software'. Finally, utility software is available to service and manage the system. This category of software is solution based, addressing issues such as security and system protection. Utility software examples include printer drivers, virus checkers and partitioning software, firewalls and disk management software, etc.

This section will give you an insight into different types of software, what it can be used for and how it can support users with specific tasks.

Operating system software

Every day computers need operating system software to function. Operating systems perform basic tasks, such as recognising input from the keyboard, sending output to the monitor or display, keeping track of files and directories on the disk, and controlling peripheral devices such as printers and scanners. In large corporate systems the operating system has an even greater responsibility in that it acts as a mediator to ensure that other programs running simultaneously do not interfere with each other. In addition, the operating system also ensures that users do not interfere with the system by restricting access to certain areas.

Operating systems can be classified into the following types:

* multi-user – allowing two or more users to run programs at the same time. In an organisation some operating systems permit hundreds or even thousands of users to run programs simultaneously
* multiprocessing – allows a program to run on more than one CPU
* multitasking – allows more than one program to operate at the same time
* multithreading – allows different parts of a single program to run at the same time
* real time – responds instantly to an input command.

Graphical user interfaces, such as Microsoft Windows 95, 98, 2000 and XP can be characterised by a number of features that include:

* a pointer – a symbol that appears on the screen that allows you to move and select objects or commands
* pointing device – such as a mouse or trackball, that enables you to select objects on the screen
* menus – most graphical user interfaces allow the user to carry out tasks and functions by selecting an option from a menu

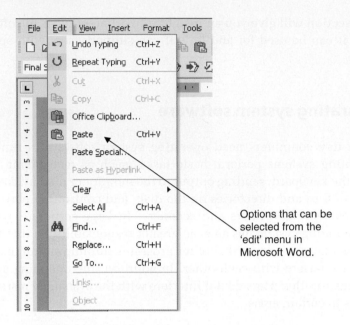

Options that can be selected from the 'edit' menu in Microsoft Word.

Figure 2.8
Sample menu items

- icons – these are miniature pictures that represent commands, files or windows. The pictures represent pictures of the actual commands, for example, a rubbish bin to represent 'rubbish' and a disk to represent 'save'. When the picture is selected the command is executed

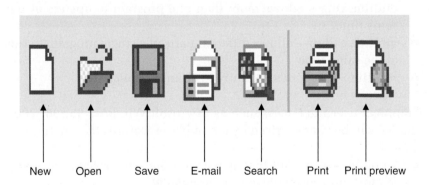

Figure 2.9
Sample icons

New   Open   Save   E-mail   Search   Print   Print preview

- desktop – this is the area on the display screen where icons are grouped. This is often referred to as the desktop because the icons are intended to represent real objects on a real desktop

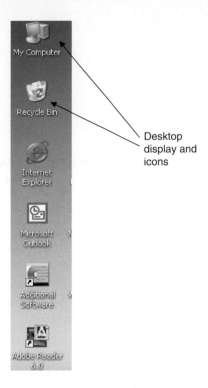

Figure 2.10

Sample desktop features

- windows – these can divide the screen into different areas. In each window, a different program or different file can be displayed.

Applications software

Applications software also enables users to interact with hardware through different text, sound, animation, video and communicative techniques.

Applications software can be defined as being general such as programs that can be accessed on the majority of computers – standard applications or bespoke. Bespoke applications are those that have been designed to meet a specific end-user requirement and have been custom designed, rather than off the shelf.

A comparison of each type can be seen in Table 2.1.

Applications software can be categorised into the following areas:

- Word processing
- Desktop publishing
- Spreadsheet

- Database
- Graphics
- Presentation
- Multimedia

Word processing

Word-processing software is quite commonly used because of its simplicity and the types of multifunctioning tasks that it can perform such as:

- Writing letters, reports and other documents
- Producing standard templates
- Producing logos and letterheads
- Mail merging documents
- Producing documents that require specific formats e.g. tables or columns
- Desktop publishing

Table 2.1

Comparison of bespoke and applications software

Bespoke software		Applications	
Benefits	**Limitations**	**Benefits**	**Limitations**
• tailored to specific requirements and can carry out specific tasks	• can take a long time to develop the software to meet an organisations needs	• can be cheaper to purchase, upgrade and maintain	• may not completely meet the needs of the end user
• can incorporate user's needs and requirements to carry out specific ICT tasks	• can be more expensive to purchase because of the development costs	• can take less time to implement because of the uniform settings	• can be of a sub-standard quality
• better quality software because it has been developed for a specific task(s)	• can be complex to use, might require retraining of the end user	• can be easier to use because of its standard features	
• may not be compatible with existing ICT systems		• compatibility with existing systems	

BTEC FIRST
INTRODUCTION TO COMPUTER SYSTEMS

APPLICATIONS SOFTWARE
Richard G. Wright
1 January 2006
A COMPARISON OF DIFFERENT TYPES OF APPLICATIONS SOFTWARE

1.0 Introduction
The introduction should provide a short summary of the overall focus and content of the report

2.0 Procedures
Identification of any procedures used to collect, collate, analyse and present information

3.0 Main findings
The main findings section is where the bulk of the report content should be placed. The main findings section should be broken down into task, action or research areas. Each area of the findings section should put forward arguments or statements supported by research and analysis. The main findings section can be broken down further into sub-sections, for example:

     3.1   Feasibility Study

           3.1.1   Fact-finding techniques
           3.1.2   Requirements analysis
           3.1.3   User analysis

4.0 Conclusions
The conclusion section should bring together all of the items discussed within the main findings section and provide a summary of the key areas identified.

5.0 Recommendations
This section is solution based, providing the subjects of the report with proposals as to how they can move forward with the report objective.

References
This section should identify and give credit for all information sources used to include; books, magazines or journals, other documents or reports, and the Internet etc.

Appendices
This section will provide supporting documentation to give additionality to the report content. Appendices could include lists of facts and figures, leaflets and downloaded information etc.

Figure 2.11

Producing standard templates – reports

Pete Kershaw

For all your building needs
The Copse
112 Windling Road
Great Haines
Norfolk
NR13 5DD

Figure 2.12

Logos and letterheads

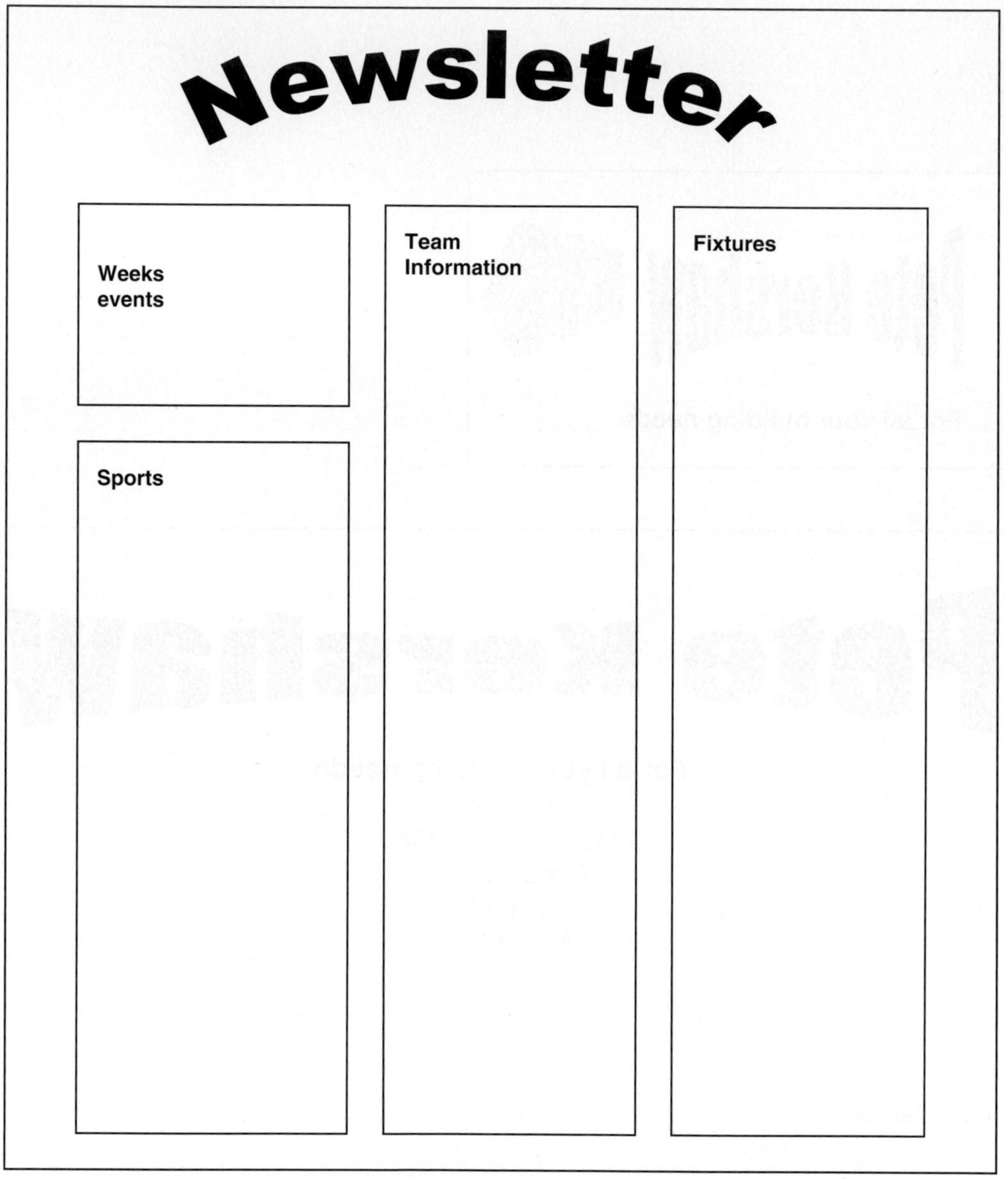

Figure 2.13

Desktop publishing example

Spreadsheets

Spreadsheets can be used to:

- Produce and display numerical, graphical and statistical data such as:
  - Sales forecasts
  - Profit and loss
  - General expenditure
  - Wage and salary information
  - Distribution facts
- Forecast information
- Calculate information

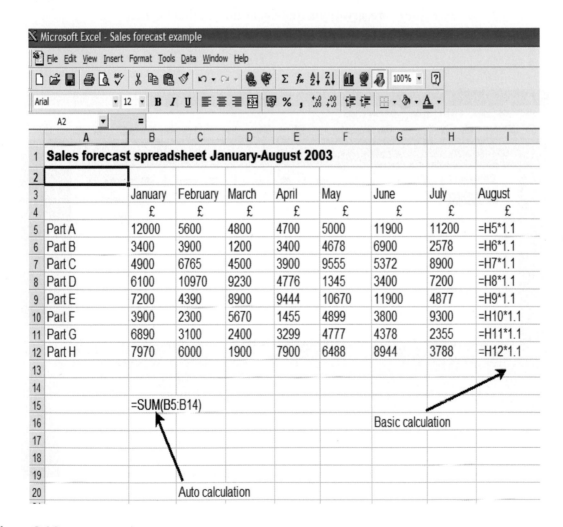

Figure 2.14

Sample spreadsheet to calculate and forecast information

- Analyse information
- Automate procedures

Databases

Database software can be used for a number of different tasks to include:

- referencing and recording (cataloguing books, CDs, videos or DVDs)
- storage of contact/customer information and other systems such as stock control, financial data, insurance claims records, etc.
- maintaining and searching for information on bookings and reservations (hotels, holidays, flights, etc.)
- retaining supplier details, membership records, etc.

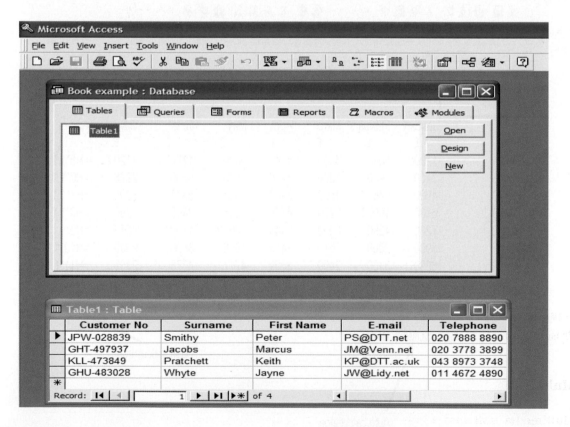

Figure 2.15

Sample database table – storage of information

Graphics

The use of graphics and graphical tools can enhance a range of documents. Graphics can be used in a number of different environments to include:

- Architectural – designing houses or housing developments
- Engineering – designing vehicles and motorised products
- Technical – designing specialist electronic products
- Scientific – designing medical, government or military products.

Graphics software can include specific design tools such as CAD (computer aided design) used in engineering, technical drawing and manufacturing environments. Graphics are associated with the design of computer games and web graphical development tools.

Presentation

Presentation software can be used to enhance the verbal delivery of a speech, talk, lecture or sales pitch, etc.

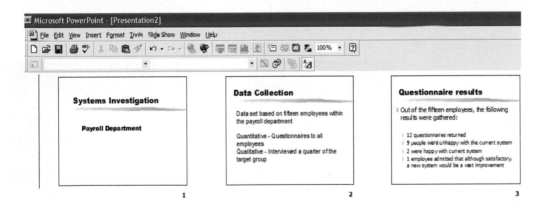

Figure 2.16
Presentation slide examples

Multimedia

Multimedia software includes the use of sound, graphics and images/moving images. The most recognised multimedia tool is that of the Internet as it incorporates each of these elements.

Utility software

This range of software provides the tools to support the operation and management of a system/computer, examples include:

- Virus checkers
- Security software e.g. firewalls
- Defragmenter software
- Partitioning software
- CD authoring
- DVD playback software

Test your knowledge

(1) What is the difference between bespoke and general applications software?
(2) Provide a description for each of the following types of software:
   - Operating system
   - Applications
   - Utility
(3) What applications software will allow you to create documents such as letters and reports?
(4) Identify three examples of what utility software can do?

Activity 5

(a) Produce a table that identifies different types of software. In the table describe what each piece of software does and give an example of each software type
(b) Using an organisation as example state how the following pieces of applications software could be used:
   - Word processing
   - Graphics
   - Spreadsheet
   - Database
   - Presentation

Health and safety and working practices

The working environment of users of ICT is of major importance when it comes to looking at issues such as health and safety. A number of issues exist that cover environmental, social and practical aspects of working conditions as shown in Figure 2.17.

Hardware connections, devices and software configuration

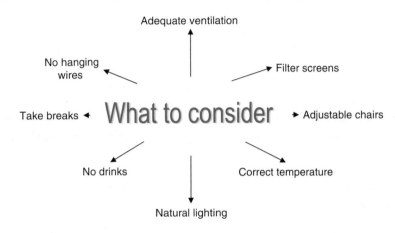

Figure 2.17
Health and safety considerations

Users should be working in an environment that has adequate ventilation and natural lighting, the temperature should also be conducive to a computing environment, especially as computers give out large quantities of heat.

Computers should also have sufficient support peripherals such as filter screens to minimise glare and height adjustable chairs. When working at a computer, no food or drink should be consumed in case liquid or crumbs fall onto the keyboard or into the case. Wires should always be packed away in appropriate conduits and not left trailing across the floor.

The best measure for health and safety in the workplace is to use common sense and adhere by standard ways of working. Organisations also offer guidelines and procedures for maintaining good working practice.

One health and safety act that has been set up to protect users of information systems and general ICT is Display Screen Equipment (VDU) Regulations 1992.

Display Screen Equipment (VDU) Regulations 1992

Under these regulations, an employer has six main obligations to fulfil. For each user and operator working in his undertaking, the employer must:

(i) assess the risks arising from their use of display screen workstations and take steps to reduce any risks identified to the 'lowest extent reasonably practicable'

(ii) ensure that new workstations ('first put into service after 1 January, 1993') meet minimum ergonomics standards set out in a schedule to the Regulations. Existing workstations have a further four years to meet the minimum requirements, provided that they are not posing a risk to their users

(iii) inform users about the results of the assessments, the actions the employer is taking and the users' entitlements under the Regulations

For each user, whether working for him or another employer (but not each operator)

(iv) plan display screen work to provide regular breaks or changes of activity

In addition, for his own employees who are users,

(v) offer eye tests before display screen use, at regular intervals and if they are experiencing visual problems. If the tests show that they are necessary and normal glasses cannot be used, then special glasses must be provided

(vi) provide appropriate health and safety training for users before display screen use or whenever the workstation is 'substantially modified'.

The need for such legislation can only benefit users and help to protect them against computer-related injuries such as:

- Repetitive Strain Injury (RSI)
- Back and upper joint problems
- Eye strain
- Exposure to radiation and hardware ozones
- Epilepsy
- Stress-related illnesses

Test your knowledge

There are a number of health and safety issues to consider when working with computer and information systems.

(1)   Identify at least one piece of legislation that protects users under the framework of 'Health and Safety at work'?
(2)   Identify four things that can improve general health and safety within an office environment?
(3)   If you were working at a computer workstation all day every day what should you do to ensure your own health and safety?
(4)   What is RSI?

What does this mean?

VDU – Visual Display Unit
DSE – Display Screen Equipment

The way that people work and working practices are very important as these not only affect what people do and how they do it but it have implications on issues such as legislation, health and safety and risk assessment.

In terms of risk assessment, there are a number of threats that impact on organisations and individual users of IT. These threats can be broken down into a number of areas that include:

(i)   Physical threats – theft of hardware, software or data
(ii)   Individual threats – users deleting or overwriting data
(iii)   Hardware threats – system crashes or processor meltdown
(iv)   Communication threats – hackers or espionage
(v)   Virus or Trojan threats – infection and propagation
(vi)   Natural threats – disasters such as fire, flood, earthquake or lightening, etc.
(vii)   Electrical surge or power-loss threat – overloading the system or rendering the system disabled
(viii) Erroneous data threats – inaccurate data in the system.

To minimise risks in an IT working environment, a number of steps can be taken. At a user level the setting up of passwords, backing up regularly, using a virus checker and firewall can all help to prevent a number of these threats. At a corporate level security policies can be drawn up to include controls such as:

(1) Access controls – identifying and authenticating users within the system, setting up passwords, building in detection tools, encrypting sensitive data
(2) Administrative controls – setting up procedures with personnel in case of a breach; disciplinary actions, defining standards and screening of personnel at the time of hiring
(3) Operations controls – back-up procedures and controlling access through smart cards, login and logout procedures and other control tools
(4) Personnel controls – creating a general awareness amongst employees, providing training and education
(5) Physical controls – secure and lock hardware, have another back-up facility off-site etc.

Once a 'working standard(s)' has been adopted, they should be formalised and communicated to everybody working within that environment.

Activity 6

You have been employed in a new role as a health and safety adminis-trator within a large insurance company. You work with employees from a range of departments including call-centre representatives, IT specialists and human resources.

(a) Design a health and safety leaflet that could be used to introduce and support new employees in their job roles
(b) Design a short presentation that focuses on the different types of legislation that protects users and holders of electronic data.

Connectivity and configurations

In terms of health and safety, computer users should be aware of how to connect and configure hardware and software safely. In terms of personal safety, for example, using static mats or wrist bands when you have the lid off a computer and you are installing a new component. Safety of data and applications should also be consid-ered making sure that correct procedures are being followed when connecting peripheral items or configuring a piece of software.

There are a number of peripheral items that can be connected to a computer. These include:

- Speakers
- Printers
- Digital cameras
- Scanners
- Web cam
- Other devices such as barcode readers or graphics tablets, etc.
- Cabling

The process of physically connecting a peripheral device is usually straightforward with the use of a cable that connects directly into the case of a computer. Following the physical connection the hardware will usually require configuration using appropriate software or selection from a menu option to ensure that the peripheral device can communicate with the computer.

Once the peripheral device has been configured, it is then ready to use.

Configuration of software can also include personalising an environment for a specific end user. This might include personalising a GUI operating system interface, for example:

- accessing toolbars
- setting up shortcuts
- changing taskbars
- adjusting the language or date/time format
- adding a screen saver
- creating a new folder structure
- allowing easy access to data.

Installation, configuration and testing system components

There are a number of initial steps and precautions that should be taken when installing hardware. These include:

(1) Shutting down and switching off you computer
(2) Unplugging the power cord from the wall socket or rear of the computer
(3) Giving yourself sufficient room to move around the computer and desk area.

Computer chips and hardware such as motherboards and hardware cards, are sensitive to static electricity. Before handling any hardware or working on the inside of the computer you should also ensure that you have discharged the static electricity from your body. At the very least you should make sure you unplug your computer from the mains and touch the bare metal case with your hand to discharge any static that may have built up in your body.

Ideally you should wear a grounding strap and/or use an anti-static mat to reduce the risk of any components being 'zapped' by static.

The majority of computers that are bought today have pre-installed applications software as part of the package. If however you need to install additional software, this can be done very easily by inserting the disk, that then launches into the step-by-step visual installation process.

If you are installing a new hard drive you should put it in a closed front bay (one that cannot be accessed from the front of the PC case). If you are installing a new CD or DVD ROM you will need to put it in an open bay which can be accessed from the front of the PC case. An open front bay is easy to locate because of the removable front panel which can be unclipped once the case is open. There may also be a metal trim which has to be snapped off before inserting the new drive.

Installing a mouse used to involve physical connection and then configuration so that the mouse and the computer could communicate with each other. These days, however, especially with a USB mouse the only real requirement is to connect the mouse physically.

In terms of installing expansion cards you would need to identify the type of slot to install your new hardware into. If you don't have a spare slot of the type you need you will have to remove one of the other cards in your computer in order to use the new one.

If you are installing the new hardware into a previously unused slot you will more than likely have to remove the backing cover from the case before you proceed. This is a metal clip or cover designed to stop dust, etc. from getting inside the case. They are normally held in place by a single screw or can be 'snapped' out of the casing using pliers. Remove the retaining screw and/or unclip the backing cover.

Printer installation and configuration involves a physical connection using a parallel, serial or USB cable. In terms of software, most printers have accompanied printer drivers that can be installed to ensure that the computer and the printer are communicating on the same level. In most modern day operating systems however, printer configurations can be selected from a list covering the majority of printer makes.

ICT systems can be configured to start-up and operate in different ways. Much of this can be controlled by the ICT system manager, however some can be configured to suit the needs of the end user, some of these configurations can include:

- Time and date set-up
- Printer, mouse and keyboard configuration
- Password properties
- Multimedia configurations
- Changes to scheduled tasks
- GUI desktop and display set-up
- Virus protection configuration
- Directory (folder) structure and settings
- Applications software icons
- Checking and setting system properties
- Power management

The majority of configurations can be carried out through the control panel on your operating system, although some such as the setting of the time and date can also be done through the ROM-BIOS start-up.

In the image featured on the control panel you can actually see how the majority of settings can be adjusted to suit user needs. These include the time and date, printer, mouse and keyboard configurations, password properties and in addition, user accounts can also be set up to protect and restrict logins to certain applications.

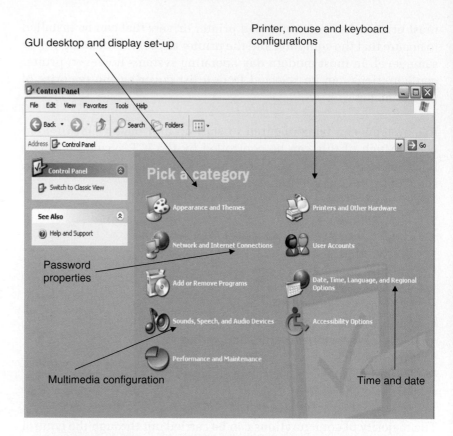

GUI desktop and display set-up

Printer, mouse and keyboard configurations

Password properties

Multimedia configuration

Time and date

Figure 2.18
Control panel overview

Figure 2.19
Time and date settings

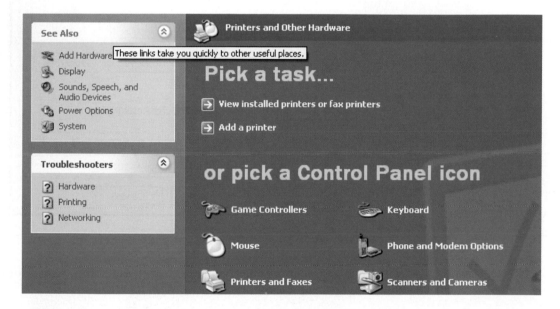

Figure 2.20

Printer configuration

Figure 2.21
Password properties

Multimedia configurations such as adjusting the graphics and sound can be addressed through the control panel.

Scheduled tasks such as backing up data, for example, can be carried out through the operating system. Depending on whether you are using a networked or stand-alone computer, the backup procedure will download your data onto a local hard disk or onto the network, where specific storage areas are designated for individual users. Most graphical operating systems procedures for carrying out scheduled tasks either involves 'point and click' or 'drag and drop'. On the performance and maintenance menu in the control panel you can also carry out a range of scheduled tasks.

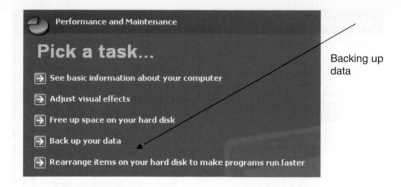

Backing up data

Figure 2.22

Performance and maintenance menu

Through the operating system you can change the way your GUI desktop and display set-up looks, this can be done through the 'Appearance and Themes' setting on the control panel.

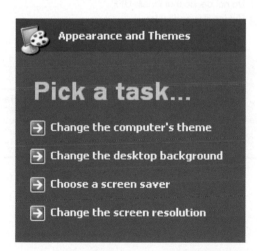

Figure 2.23

Appearance and themes menu

Virus protection software can be installed or downloaded from the Internet and configured to start-up every time you boot up your computer. Reminders will also be activated to enable you to check and update the version and level of virus protection at regular intervals.

Access to directories and folders can be gained from the 'start' menu in operating systems such as Windows, where you can look into 'My Computer' or 'My Documents' to locate directories and folders. In addition, 'Folder Options' can also be viewed through the control panel.

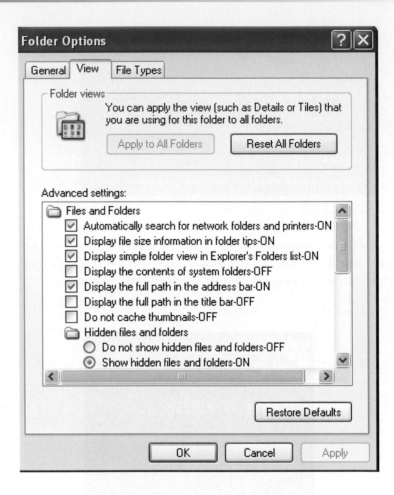

Figure 2.24

Directory folder structure
and settings

Applications software icons can be changed through the 'Properties' function – by right-clicking on the icon. In addition, icons can be downloaded and used as a replacement of the ones that are supplied with the operating system.

Figure 2.25

Application software – traditional icons

Checking and setting system properties – such as running diagnostics can also be carried out through your desktop and control panel. Viewing information about your computer, such as 'checking how much space is available on your hard disk' through 'Properties':

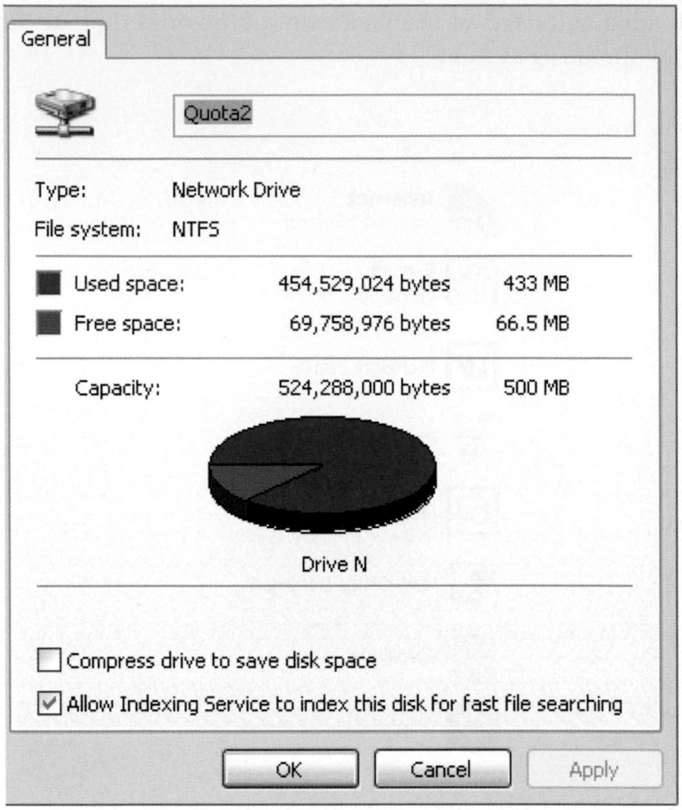

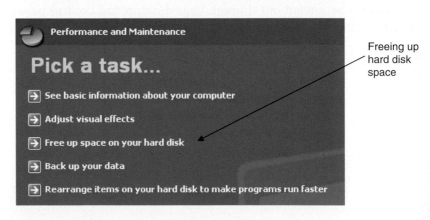

Figure 2.26

Checking space
availability

Freeing up space on your hard disk to address this is one example.

Figure 2.27

Freeing up hard disk
space

Changing the screen resolution of your monitor is also another
example of checking and setting system properties.

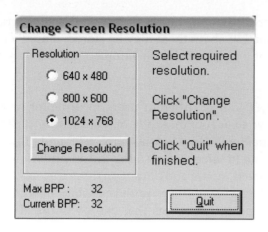

Figure 2.28

Screen resolution
dialogue box

Power management functions that control your ability to logoff,
switch between users and shut down can be accessed through the
'start' menu.

Figure 2.29

Power management
functions

Activity 7

(a) Using applications software of your choice, configure it to
include preparing or setting items such as:
  • Preferences (or configuration files)
  • Data templates and macros
  • Saving and backup security
  • Menus, toolbars and buttons
  • Directory structures and defaults

(b) Keep a record of how you have configured the applications software (set out a step-by-step guide) that another end user could
follow

(c) Keep a log of any problems that you have encountered during
the configuration activity.

Systems security

To protect organisations, users of ICT and the general public for whom information about them may be stored, a number of measures and a range of legislation can be enforced and used as a controlling measure.

Legislation can impact different users in different ways. Organisations will have to ensure that they operate within certain legislative boundaries that include informing employees and third parties about how they intend to safeguard systems and any information collected, processed, copied, stored and output on these systems. Personal users will need to be aware of the required legislation, what their responsibilities are and the penalties that can be imposed if any laws or regulations are breached.

The types of legislation that an organisation would need to consider would effect everyday operations in terms of:

* Collecting, processing and storing data
* Using software
* Protecting their employees and ensuring that working conditions are of an acceptable standard.

Data Protection Act 1984 and 1988

The Data Protection Act applies to the processing of data and information by any source, either electronic or paper based. The act places obligations on people who collect, process and store personal records and data about consumers or customers. The act is based upon a set of principles which binds a user or an organisation into following a set of procedures offering assurances that data is kept secure.

The main principles include:

(1) Personal data shall be processed fairly and lawfully and, in particular, shall not be processed unless:
   * At least one of the conditions in Schedule 2 of the 1998 Act is met, and
   * In the case of sensitive personal data, at least one of the conditions in Schedule 3 of the 1998 Act is also met
(2) Personal data shall be obtained only for one or more specified and lawful purposes, and shall not be further processed in any manner incompatible with that purpose or those purposes
(3) Personal data shall be adequate, relevant and not excessive in relation to the purpose or purposes for which they are processed

(4) Personal data shall be accurate and, where necessary, kept up-to-date

(5) Personal data processed for any purpose or purposes shall not be kept for longer than is necessary for that purpose or those purposes

(6) Personal data shall be processed in accordance with the rights of data subjects under this Act

(7) Appropriate technical and organisational measures shall be taken against unauthorised or unlawful processing of personal data and against accidental loss or destruction of, or damage to, personal data

(8) Personal data shall not be transferred to a country or territory outside the EEA (European Economic Area) unless that country or territory ensures an adequate level of protection for the rights and freedom of data subjects in relation to the processing of personal data.

The Act gives rights to individuals in respect of personal data held about them by data controllers. These include the rights:

- To make subject access requests about the nature of the information and to discover to whom it has been disclosed
- To prevent processing likely to cause damage or distress
- To prevent processing for the purposes of direct marketing
- To be informed about the mechanics of any automated decision-taking process that will significantly affect them
- Not to have significant decisions that affect them made solely by an automated decision-taking process
- To take action for compensation if they suffer damage by any contravention of the Act by the data controller
- To take action to rectify, block, erase or destroy inaccurate data
- To request the Commissioner to make an assessment as to whether any provision of the Act has been contravened.

The Act does provide wide exemptions for journalistic, artistic, or literary purposes that would otherwise be in breach of the law.

What does this mean?

Personal data:	Information about living, identifiable individuals. Personal data does not have to be particularly sensitive information and can be as little as name and address
Data users:	Those who control the contents, and use of, a collection of personal data. They can be any type of company or organisation, large or small, within the public or private sector. A data user can also be a sole trader, partnership or an individual. A data user need not necessarily own a computer
Data subjects:	The individuals to whom the personal data relates

The role of the Data Protection Commissioner

The Commissioner is an independent supervisory authority and has an international role as well as a national one. Primarily the Commissioner is responsible for ensuring that the Data Protection legislation is enforced.

In the UK, the Commission has a range of duties which include:

• Promotion of good information handling
• Encouraging codes of practice for data controllers.

In order to carry out these duties the Commissioner maintains a public register of data controllers. Each register entry contains details about the controller such as their name, address and a description of the processing of the personal data to be carried out.

Registering entries   All users, with a few exceptions have to register an entry/entries giving their name, address and broad descriptions of:

• those about whom personal data are held
• the items of data held
• the purposes for which the data are used
• the sources from which the information may be disclosed i.e. shown or passed to

- any overseas countries or territories to which the data may be transferred.

Computer Misuse Act 1990

The Computer Misuse Act was enforced to address the increased threat of hackers trying to gain unauthorised access to a computer system. Prior to this Act there was minimal protection and difficulties in prosecuting because theft of data by hacking was not considered as deprivation to the owner. There a number of offences and penalties under this Act, these include:

Offences

- Unauthorised access – an attempt by a hacker to gain unauthorised access to a computer system
- Unauthorised access, with the intention of committing another offence – on gaining access, a hacker will then continue with the intent of committing a further crime
- Unauthorised modification of data or programs – introducing viruses to a computer system is a criminal offence. Guilt is assessed by the level of intent to cause disruption, or to impair the processes of a computer system.

Penalties

- Unauthorised access – imprisonment for up to six months and/or a fine of up to £2,000
- Unauthorised access with the intention of committing another offence – imprisonment for up to five years and/or an unlimited fine
- Unauthorised modification – imprisonment for up to five years and/or an unlimited fine.

Copyright

Copyright is awarded to a product or brand following its completion no further action is required in order to activate it. Copyright is transferable if the originator/author grants it and it can exist for up to fifty years following the death of the originator/author.

In conjunction with software a number of copyright issues exist. First, software piracy – the copying of software to be used on more machines than individual licences have been paid for.

Second, ownership – if a bespoke piece of software has been developed for an organisation, the copyright remains with the developer unless conditions have been written into a contract. Finally transference – can an employee who has developed a piece of software for their organisation take the ownership and copyright with them to another. Again unless this is addressed in the employees contract the organisation will have no right to any software developed.

The Federation Against Software Theft (FAST) was set up in 1984 by the software industry with the aim of preventing software piracy. Anybody caught breaching the copyright law would be prosecuted under this federation.

Copyright, Designs and Patents Act

The Copyright, Designs and Patents Act provides protection to software developers and organisations against unauthorised copying of their software, designs, printed material and any other product. Under copyright legislation, an organisation or developer can ensure that its Intellectual Property Rights (IPR) has been safeguarded against third parties who wish to exploit and make gains from the originator's research and developments.

Software piracy and misuse

Software piracy can be broken down into a number of key areas, these include:

- Recordable CD-ROMs – pirates compiling large amounts of software onto one recordable CD-ROM and making multiple copies of the CD-ROM
- Professional counterfeits – these are professionally made copies of software including media, packages, licences and even security holograms. They are made to resemble the genuine article
- Internet piracy – the downloading or distribution of software on the Internet infringing any copyright
- Corporate overuse – where organisations install a software package/s onto more machines than they have licences for
- Hard disk loaders – where retail outlets or dealers who load infringing versions of software onto a computer system to encourage customers into buying their computer hardware. Customers will not have the appropriate licences or be entitled to other services such as technical support or upgrades.

There are a number of methods that can be used to enforce and control:

(a) Data protection legislation
(b) Software misuse legislation
(c) Health and safety legislation

These are illustrated in Table 2.2.

Table 2.2

Methods of enforcing and controlling legislation within an organisation

Data protection legislation	<ul><li>have a departmental data protection officer</li><li>detailed job descriptions</li><li>have procedures to follow-up any anomalies</li><li>incorporate security measures such as the setting up of passwords, physical logins, firewalls, encryption</li><li>have a strict code of practice with regards to personal databases and software, etc.</li><li>educate employees</li><li>disciplinary procedures</li><li>use of access level</li><li>network activity logging</li></ul>
Software misuse	<ul><li>do not permit employees to install unauthorised or unlicensed software</li><li>do not permit employees to copy software for home or unlicensed use</li><li>ensure that the organisation has a corporate hardware/software policy</li><li>ensure that virus scanning takes place</li><li>initiate regular audits</li></ul>
Health and safety	<ul><li>have a health and safety officer</li><li>regular inspections of work stations against health, safety and ergonomic criteria</li><li>train staff – correct use of hardware, software and legislation regarding health and safety issues</li><li>procedures for ensuring that faulty equipment is replaced</li><li>initiatives and the promotion of good health and safety practice</li><li>disciplinary procedures</li></ul>

Test your knowledge

(1) Why will legislation have an impact upon users of ICT?
(2) What are the important features of the Data Protection Act?
(3) What does the Computer Misuse Act cover?
(4) Why do you need Copyright laws?

Security threats and issues

There are a number of security issues to consider when working with ICT systems. To protect organisations, users and the general public for whom information about them may be stored, a number of measures and guidelines have been introduced that fall broadly into two categories:

(i) Data security
(ii) Data protection

Although these two issues are closely related, data security examines the area of physical security issues and data protection looks at the measures that have been introduced to protect consumer data.

Keeping data secure can be quite difficult because of the environment in which users work and levels of user and access requirements to the data. With the movement towards a totally networked environment promoting a culture of 'sharing' the issue of data security is even more important and should be addressed at a number of levels, as shown in Figure 2.30.

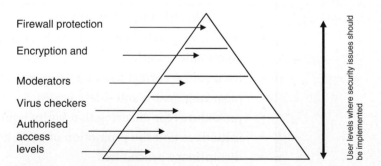

Figure 2.30

Levels of security

As illustrated security measures need to be integrated at each user level within an organisation. The indication of security measure does not confine it to a certain level but reflects on an organisational scale what should be implemented and the scale of implementation. In addition to these proposed security measures, the issue of physical security also exists – ensuring that hardware and software is kept physically secure under lock and key.

The actual protection of data can be resolved quite easily by introducing good practice measures such as backing up all data to a secondary storage device and limiting file access, imposing restrictions to read only, execute only read/write. However data protection is also covered more widely under certain Acts such as the Data Protection Act 1984.

Firewall protection

The primary aim of a firewall is to guard against unauthorised access to an internal network. In effect, a firewall is a gateway with a lock, the gateway only opens for information packets that pass one or more security inspections.

There are three basic types of firewalls, these include:

(i) Application gateways – the first gateways are sometimes referred to as proxy gateways. These are made up of hosts that run special software to act as a proxy server. Clients behind the firewall must know how to use the proxy, and be configured to do so in order to use Internet services. This software runs at the 'application layer' of the ISO/OSI Reference Model, hence the name. Traditionally application gateways have been the most secure, because they do not allow anything to pass by default, but need to have the programs written and turned on in order to begin passing traffic.

(ii) Packet filtering – is a technique whereby routers have 'access control lists' turned on. By default, a router will pass all traffic sent to it, and will do so without any sort of restrictions. Access control is performed at a lower ISO/OSI layer (typically, the transport or session layer). Due to the fact that packet filtering is done with routers, it is often much faster than application gateways.

(iii) Hybrid system – a mixture between application gateways and packet filtering. In some of these systems, new connections must be authenticated and approved at the application layer. Once this has been done, the remainder of the connection is passed down to the session layer, where packet filters watch the connection to ensure that only packets that are part of an ongoing (already authenticated and approved) conversation are being passed.

Encryption and filtering software

Encryption software scrambles message transmissions – when a message is encrypted, a secret numerical code is applied 'encryption key', the message can be transmitted or stored in indecipherable characters. The message can only be read after it has been reconstructed through the use of a 'matching key'.

Moderators

Moderators have the responsibility of controlling, filtering and restricting information that gets shared across a network.

Virus checkers

These programs are designed to search for viruses, notify users of their existence and remove them from infected files or disks.

Authorised access levels and passwords

On a networked system various privilege levels can be set up to restrict users access to shared resources such as files, folders, printers and other peripheral devices. A password system can also be implemented to divide levels of entry in accordance to job role and information requirements.

For example, a finance assistant may need access to personnel data when generating the monthly payroll. Data about employees however, may be password protected by personnel in the human resources department – so special permissions may be required to gain entry to this data.

Audit control software will allow an organisation to monitor and record what they have on their network at a point in time and provide them with an opportunity to check that what they have on their system has been authorised and is legal.

Over a period of time a number of factors could impact upon how much software an organisation acquires without their knowledge.

These can include:

- Illegal copying of software by employees
- Downloading of software by employees
- Installation of software by employees
- Exceeded licence use of software.

These interventions by employees may occur with little or no consideration to the organisation and its responsibility to ensure that software is not been misused or abused.

User rights and file permissions

Within certain IT systems, users are given permissions to access some areas of a folder, application or document and be restricted from others. By allowing users certain rights within a given system, security of data can be reassured and the span of control can be limited. An example of this can be seen in the case of an IT system in a doctor's surgery. The administration staff may have access to appointments and scheduling, the nurses may have access to patient information and the GP could have full access and rights to print out prescriptions and authorise medication.

In addition certain permissions may also be set up to allow certain users partial access to a file, so for example, information can be read (read only), but not written to or users may be able to run a program (execute only) but not view it. Users with full read/write permissions would be able to view, update, amend and delete accordingly.

Management Issues

Risk analysis examines how liable an organisation is open to security breaches based on their current security provisions.

Risk analysis can identify the elements of an information system, assess the value of each element to the business, identify any threats upon that element and assess the likelihood of that threat occurring.

Threats that can occur can be broken down into a number of areas that include:

- Physical threats – theft of hardware, software or data
- Personnel threats – staff members deleting or overwriting data
- Hardware threats – system crashes or processor meltdown

- Communication threats – hackers or espionage
- Virus or Trojan threats – infection and propagation
- Natural threats – disasters such as fire, flood, earthquake or lightening, etc.
- Electrical surge or power loss threat – overloading the system or rendering the system disabled
- Erroneous data threats – inaccurate data in the system.

Once potential threats and risks have been identified, policies can be put in place to address them. A corporate ICT security policy can be drawn up to address such threats, typical content to include:

(1) Access controls – identifying and authenticating users within the system, setting up passwords, building in detection tools, encrypting sensitive data
(2) Administrative controls – setting up procedures with personnel in case of a breach; disciplinary actions, defining standards and screening of personnel at the time of hiring
(3) Operations controls – backup procedures and controlling access through smart cards, login and logout procedures and other control tools
(4) Personnel controls – creating a general awareness amongst employees, providing training and education
(5) Physical controls – secure and lock hardware, have another back-up facility off-site, etc.

Corporate information systems security policy

Contingency plans can be used to combat potential and actual threats to a system. The majority of organisations will have an adopted security policy that employees would be aware of, the plan and policy being open to continuous review and updating.

The structure of a contingency plan would be unique to an organisation and their requirements.

Some organisations are more at risk than others depending upon:

- Their size
- Location
- Proximity to known natural disasters and threats – flood areas etc.
- Core business activity.

A strategy based on recovery recognises that no system is infallible.

Disaster recovery plans

As a result, a number of companies have emerged providing 'disaster recovery' services if no internal organisation contingency plan has been drawn up. These companies will maintain copies of important data and files on behalf of an organisation.

A disaster recovery plan can include a provision for backing-up facilities in the event of a disaster. These provisions can include:

- Subscribing to a disaster recovery service
- An arrangement with a company that runs compatible computer systems
- A secondary backup site that is distanced geographically from the original
- Use of multiple servers.

Some large organisations may have a 'backup site' so that data processing can be switched to a secondary site immediately in the case of an emergency. Smaller organisations might employ other measures such as RAID or data warehousing facilities.

Test your knowledge

(1)   What security measures can be enforced within an organisation?
(2)   What is meant by the term 'risk analysis'?
(3)   Why are some organisations more at risk than others in terms of potential threats to their systems?
(4)   What measures can a large and a small company take to protect their data?

Chapter 3

Website development

This unit will provide students with an understanding about why websites are developed, the purpose of design and technologies used.

In addition this unit will explore the growing potential of websites in terms of how they have emerged in this new technological era, what their purpose is and the unlimited boundaries in terms of accessing, developing and using them as an information portal, marketing and promotional source and a selling tool.

Website design has become a growing business at all levels, with many skills being developed at school and in further education. With a range of software available to support the design of pages, many teenagers have already experimented, and in some cases have designed their own personal web page within a matter of weeks.

The use of text, graphics, sound, moving images and links has turned website design into a very profitable and affordable source of branding for organisations across the world, from small corner shops through to multinational corporations.

When you complete this unit you should be able to:

(1) Understand purposes of websites and the laws and guidelines that concern their development
(2) Understand the principles of multi-page website design
(3) Be able to create a multi-page website.

Why do we need websites?

Websites have a wide range of functions that are suited to all types of end users. Websites can be designed to meet a specific purpose such as distributing information or they can be used generally as a tool for promoting a product, service, brand or company.

Activity 1

The purpose of websites is dependent upon the type of user or organisation and the message that they want to convey to their audience.

(a) Complete the table by providing two examples for each purpose listed

Purpose	Organisation/user type	Web address	How it is achieved
Provide information on education and training courses			
Provide information on CD and DVD prices			
Provide financial information			
Provide information on holidays and flights			

(b) Provide a short review of how easy or difficult you found it to find the appropriate websites.

A website can be designed for a specific purpose but also have multifunctional uses as shown in Figure 3.1.

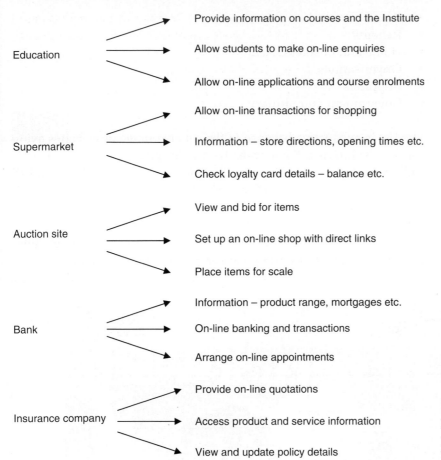

Figure 3.1

Multifunctional purposes of specific websites

Some of the main reasons for setting up a website include:

* Promotion of a product, service, brand, image
* An information portal
* Provide on-line transaction and booking facilities
* Provide advice and guidance – medical sites etc.
* Provide an interactive communication community – chat sites, forums and user groups, etc.
* Provide on-line interactive social and leisure activities – on-line games, e.g. role playing, chess, scrabble, etc.

Websites and client needs

Websites are designed for a particular set of end users, these could include:

* Potential and existing customers
* Students and teachers

- Employees and employers
- Patients
- Home and business users
- Organisations
- Suppliers
- Government and military

The list is exhaustive because of the diverse range of websites available on the Internet. Some websites are designed with a very specific end user category, for example, the BBC CBeebies website as shown in Figure 3.2 is aimed at children.

Other websites also have particular users that they want to market to, for example, The Training and Education Company promotes their website to educate and train users as shown in Figure 3.3.

Figure 3.2

CBeebies website. www.bbc.co.uk/cbeebies/

Figure 3.3

The Training and Education Company. www.train-ed.co.uk

Apart from the overall purpose of websites meeting a specific end user need, there are other areas to be considered when designing a website. From a user's perspective, these include as shown below.

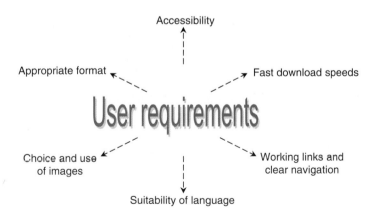

The easier or more memorable a website is to locate the greater the chance that users will refer to it again and use that site over another less accessible site. There are a number of ways that websites can become accessible. One method is to register with a search engine

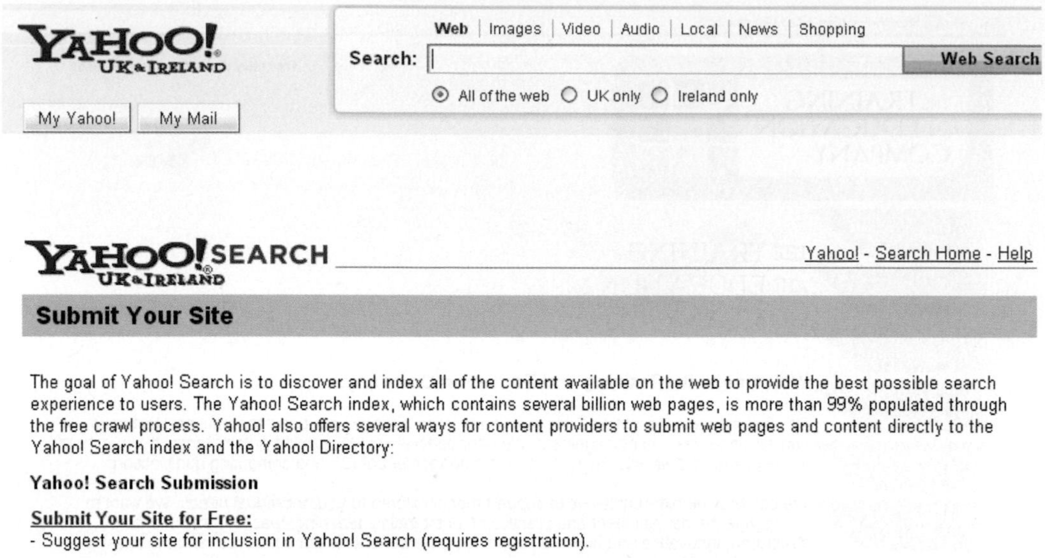

Figure 3.4

Yahoo search engine and site submission. www.yahoo.com

such as Yahoo. Your website can be submitted directly for inclusion in Yahoo as shown in Figure 3.4.

Another method if you want to register a website with a number of search engines is to submit a list of keywords that are relevant to your website. For example, a website offering CDs and DVDs for sale might submit keywords such as:

'CD, DVD, Chart, Region 2, Region 1, Pop, R&B, Classical, Music, Film, Comedy, Drama, TV, Film, Sci-fi, Thriller, Cheap prices'

Therefore a user searching for a website that supplies CDs and DVDs might use a combination of these keywords to find what they need.

In terms of accessibility registering a meaningful or memorable website address is also important because sometimes you can guess the web address by the company name, for example:

Microsoft	– www.microsoft.com
eBay	– www.ebay.co.uk
The Carphone Warehouse	– www.thecarphonewarehouse.com
BBC	– www.bbc.co.uk
Amazon	– www.amazon.co.uk

Depending upon the type of communications device being used, for example, a modem, ADSL, ISDN or cable, etc. this can impact upon how long it takes to download a website. In conjunction, the larger the website the longer it will take to display or download.

Working links and clear navigation through a website is another need from an end user's perspective as shown in Figure 3.5. A website where the links do not work or command buttons that do not navigate you to another area of the website makes it almost ineffective.

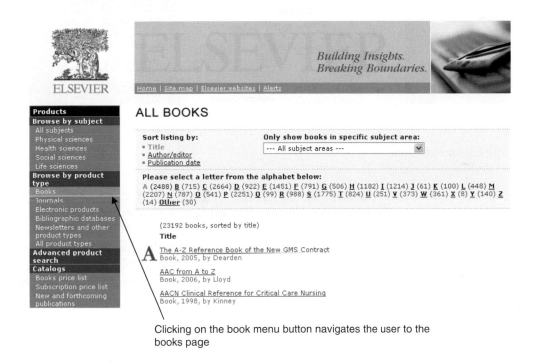

Clicking on the book menu button navigates the user to the books page

Figure 3.5

Navigation through a website

Some websites may have built-in language translators to facilitate users in being able to access and understand the page contents.

The choice and use of images can again be dependent upon the type of message that needs to be conveyed. Sites for children tend to have an abundance of graphics and colour, the graphics themselves being the links to other areas of the website as shown in Figure 3.6.

The format of a website is extremely important in terms of the colour, font and layout. As seen in the example page in Figure 3.6, the format of a site can be very specific to the type of audience and can therefore

Figure 3.6

Use of graphics on websites

be dictated by lots of colour, good use of images and a uncluttered format, making it easy for children to access and use.

Another good example is that of eBay that has a very clear and structured format that guides users to individual sections of the auction and provides search facilities to allow for easy navigation, as shown in Figures 3.7 and 3.8.

Laws, legislation and guidelines that can affect website development

Legislation can impact different users in different ways. Organisations will have to ensure that they operate within certain legislative boundaries that include informing employees and third parties about how they intend to safeguard systems and any information collected, processed, copied, stored and output on these systems. Personal users will need to be aware of the required legislation, what their responsibilities are and the penalties that can be imposed if any laws or regulations are breached.

There is a wide range of legislation that can be used to protect materials and the original content of websites and data and information, in general. Some of these include:

- Data Protection Act 1998
- Copyright Designs and Patents Act 1988
- Digital Millennium Copyright Act 2000

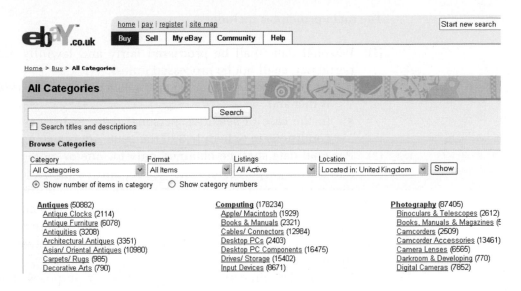

Figure 3.7

Search facilities

Figure 3.8

Easy navigation to particular auctions

Data Protection Act 1988

The Data Protection Act applies to the processing of data and information by any source, either electronic or paper based. The act places obligations on people who collect, process and store personal records and data about consumers or customers. The act is based upon a set of principles which binds a user or an organisation into following a set of procedures offering assurances that data is kept secure.

The main principles include:

(1) Personal data shall be processed fairly and lawfully and, in particular, shall not be processed unless:
- At least one of the conditions in Schedule 2 of the 1998 Act is met and
- In the case of sensitive personal data, at least one of the conditions in Schedule 3 of the 1998 Act is also met

(2) Personal data shall be obtained only for one or more specified and lawful purposes, and shall not be further processed in any manner incompatible with that purpose or those purposes

(3) Personal data shall be adequate, relevant, and not excessive in relation to the purpose or purposes for which they are processed

(4) Personal data shall be accurate and, where necessary, kept up-to-date

(5) Personal data processed for any purpose or purposes shall not be kept for longer than is necessary for that purpose or those purposes

(6) Personal data shall be processed in accordance with the rights of data subjects under this Act

(7) Appropriate technical and organisational measures shall be taken against unauthorised or unlawful processing of personal data and against accidental loss or destruction of, or damage to, personal data

(8) Personal data shall not be transferred to a country or territory outside the EEA (European Economic Area) unless that country or territory ensures an adequate level of protection for the rights and freedom of data subjects in relation to the processing of personal data.

The Act gives rights to individuals in respect of personal data held about them by data controllers. These include the rights:

- To make subject access requests about the nature of the information and to discover to whom it has been disclosed
- To prevent processing likely to cause damage or distress
- To prevent processing for the purposes of direct marketing
- To be informed about the mechanics of any automated decision-taking process that will significantly affect them
- Not to have significant decisions that affect them made solely by an automated decision-taking process
- To take action for compensation if they suffer damage by any contravention of the Act by the data controller
- To take action to rectify, block, erase or destroy inaccurate data
- To request the Commissioner to make an assessment as to whether any provision of the Act has been contravened.

The Act does provide wide exemptions for journalistic, artistic or literary purposes that would otherwise be in breach of the law.

What does this mean?

Personal data:	Information about living, identifiable individuals. Personal data does not have to be particularly sensitive information and can be as little as name and address
Data users:	Those who control the contents, and use of, a collection of personal data. They can be any type of company or organisation, large or small, within the public or private sector.
	A data user can also be a sole trader, partnership, or an individual. A data user need not necessarily own a computer
Data subjects:	The individuals to whom the personal data relates
Automatically processed:	Processed by computer or other technology such as documents image-processing systems

The role of the Data Protection Commissioner

The Commissioner is an independent supervisory authority and has an international role as well as a national one. Primarily the Commissioner is responsible for ensuring that the Data Protection legislation is enforced.

In the UK, the Commission has a range of duties to include:

- Promotion of good information handling
- Encouraging codes of practice for data controllers.

In order to carry out these duties the Commissioner maintains a public register of data controllers. Each register entry contains details about the controller such as their name, address and a description of the processing of the personal data to be carried out.

Registering entries

All users, with a few exceptions have to register an entry/entries giving their name, address and broad descriptions of:

- those about whom personal data are held
- the items of data held
- the purposes for which the data are used
- the sources from which the information may be disclosed i.e. shown or passed to
- any overseas countries or territories to which the data may be transferred.

Copyright, Designs and Patents Act 1988

The Copyright, Designs and Patents Act provides protection to software developers and organisations against unauthorised copying of their software, designs, printed material and any other product. Under copyright legislation, an organisation or developer can ensure that its Intellectual Property Rights (IPR) has been safeguarded against third parties who wish to exploit and make gains from the originators research and developments.

Digital Millennium Copyright Act (DMCA)

The DMCA was signed into law by President Clinton on 28 October, 1998. The DMCA implements two former 1996 World Intellectual Property Organisation treaties – the Copyright Treaty and the Performances and Phonograms Treaty. What this means is that work posted on the Internet by the original author is protected by the Copyright Act and may also be subject to further protection under the DMCA.

Violation of the DMCA can result in a range of civil penalties to include:

- temporary and permanent injunctions
- impounding of any device or product that was involved in a violation
- statutory or actual damages
- costs

- reasonable legal fees if you are successful with any lawsuit
- destruction of any device involved in the violation of the DMCA.

On a larger scale, criminal penalties can also be imposed.

Corporate policies and Codes of Practice

Another mechanism that an organisation can use in conjunction with legislation is to draw up a corporate policy or have a Code of Practice regarding the use of the Internet and guidelines for employers about what is and is not acceptable at work.

A Code of Practice provides a set of guidelines about the standards and quality of work to be undertaken by employees within an organisation. The code is intended to ensure that a high level of professionalism is maintained when working within organisations. A Code of Practice contains a number of elements, these can include:

- responsibilities for the use and control of the Internet or company intranet system
- responsibilities for use of company hardware and software
- responsibilities for the use of data
- responsibilities for the correct use of time
- authorisation in terms of security, passwords and access rights, etc. depending upon the level of the employee
- the implementation of legislation such as the Data Protection Act.

A Code of Practice does help to clarify the expectations and behaviour of employees and employers on a professional level at work. This code is not part of the legislative procedure; however it is still enforceable within organisations. Within organisations, the need for this code is important so that issues of abusing resources in work-time are addressed and boundaries are set and agreed by both parties.

Principles of website design

Before you start to design a website, there are a number of things that you need to consider. Some of these considerations will be dependent upon the purpose and function of the website – who the website is being designed for, what their requirements are and who the target audience will be. Other considerations will be based upon certain constraints such as, the skills and ability of the designer, time and cost.

Prior to any physical design there are a number of steps that should be taken.

Step One

Identify/analyse why there is a need for a website

→ Have you been asked to design one for a client or customer or is the design driven by a personal need?

Step Two

Identify the function/purpose of the website

→ Is it to promote a product or service, is it to provide information and guidance, is it to allow for on-line transactions etc.?

Step Three

Consider any constraints

→ Is there limited time, small budget and access to other resources etc.?

Step Four

Assess own skill and knowledge base

→ What is the extent of your web design skills, beginner, intermediate, advanced level – as this will determine the complexity of the design and whether or not you can meet the end user requirements?

Step Five

Decide on the tools to be used in the design

⌐⟶ Will you use an on-line website builder (some of which are free), an off-line builder that include packages such as Dreamweaver or Frontpage, or by yourself using a language such as html (hypertext mark-up language)?

Step Six

Check if the website needs to comply with a prescribed corporate colour, layout or image

⌐⟶ If you are designing a website for a third party there may be some restrictions in terms of the choice of colours, graphics or even layout that will impact upon the overall design

Step Seven

Prepare draft designs

⌐⟶ Prior to any physical computer-based web design, a draft of the pages and proposed content should be produced. This could be on a storyboard basis or just page-by-page designs

Step Eight

Confirm and sign-off the proposed designs

It is essential to get the draft designs approved and signed-off before embarking on the physical build. Again if the website is for personal use, you need to ensure that you are happy with the content and format before going ahead with the design

By following the eight-step design plan, it should ensure that any issues are addressed sooner rather than later in the build.

Web page construction features

There are a number of ways that a website can be designed. If you are using HTML you can create a page(s) offline and then upload them to your Internet Service Provider (ISP) via File Transfer Protocol (FTP). Or you could create your web page(s) online using a Telnet program and accessing UNIX.

If a page(s) is being created offline, it can be done with the use of any text editing or word processing document. By saving the document, as a 'text', 'plain text' or 'text only' document will ensure that it is read properly by a web browser. Once created, the page(s) will then need to be uploaded onto the server. UNIX will allow you to create your page(s) online.

Whatever method you choose to use, there are various construction features that need to be taken into consideration such as frames, action buttons and links, download speeds and interactive features such as registration logon, e-mail links, etc.

Some of the more common construction features can be illustrated in the following website examples.

Frames are used to organise a page into sections that can easily be updated as shown in Figure 3.9.

Action buttons and links are used frequently in multi-page website to aid navigation through a site as shown in Figure 3.10.

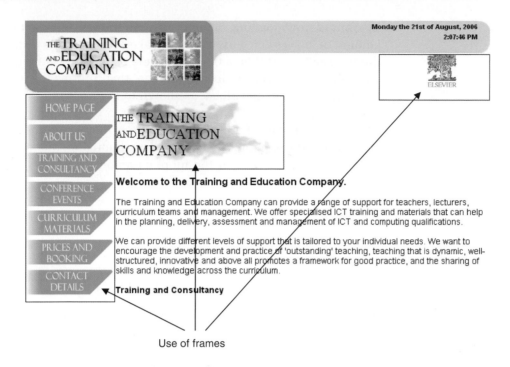

Use of frames

Figure 3.9

Example of frames

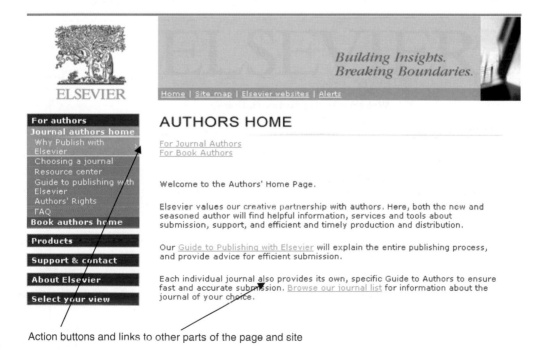

Action buttons and links to other parts of the page and site

Figure 3.10

Example of action buttons and links

In terms of downloading, depending upon the size of the site and the amount of images being used it could take a few seconds to download the information. If this is the case, some organisations tend to have an initial start-up screen 'loading screen' that informs the user about the progress of the download, as shown in Figure 3.11.

There are a range of interactive features that should be considered when developing a website. The inclusion of e-mail links and login areas are two of the more common features as shown in Figure 3.12.

WELCOME TO

THE **TRAINING**
AND **EDUCATION**
COMPANY

Figure 3.11

Example of a download screen

PLEASE WAIT WHILE THE WEBSITE LOADS
THIS WILL ONLY TAKE A FEW SECONDS

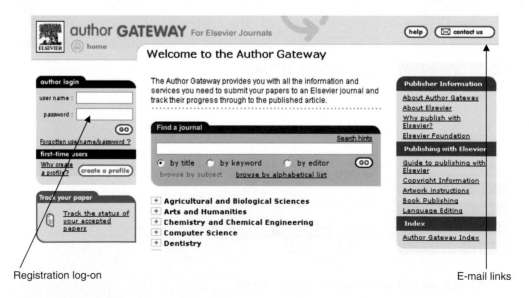

Registration log-on

E-mail links

Figure 3.12

Example registration logon screen and e-mail links

We have explored the eight steps that should be addressed prior to any web build. Thus ensuring that the website meets the required need, is fully supported in terms of the necessary resources and that drafts are approved before embarking on the physical design.

The options available to a designer are quite extensive depending upon the existing level of knowledge and skills, money and time.

Designing a website can be approached in a number of ways to include:

(1) Use of a specialist package such as Microsoft Frontpage or Macromedia's Dreamweaver
(2) Use of HTML
(3) Use of on-line software that requires minimal input from the designer as the underlying build is carried out by a third party
(4) Embedded software or use of other tools such as 'Flash'.

Creating a multi-page website

Using a specialist package

This next section will explore one particular specialist web design package – Frontpage. The section will introduce to the basic tools, techniques and functions and provide some guidance on how to develop a web page.

Frontpage main screen

Menu bar

Formatting toolbar

Standard toolbar

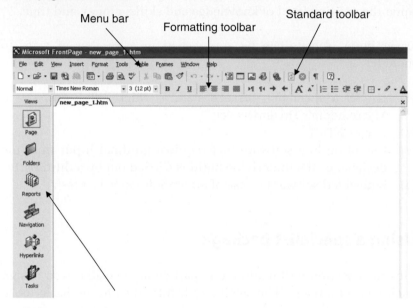

View options

View tabs

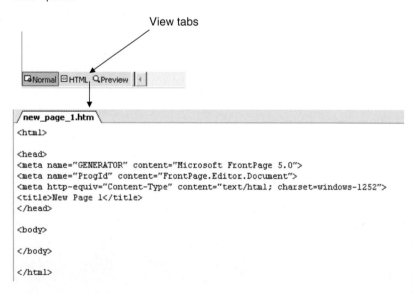

Figure 3.13

Frontpage initial screens

Views available in frontpage

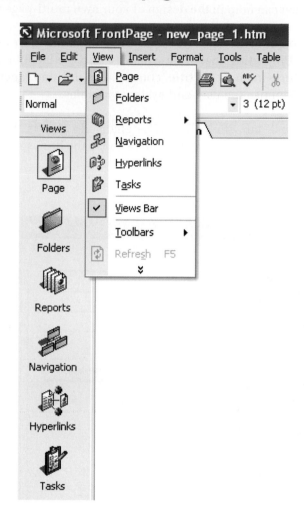

Figure 3.14
Views available

- **Page view** gives you a 'what you see is what you get' (WYSIWYG) editing environment for creating and editing web pages
- **Folders view** lists all of the files and folders in your web for easy management
- **Reports view** identifies any problems with the pages and links in the web pages including slow-loading pages, broken links, and other errors
- **Navigation view** lists the navigation order of the site and allows you to change the order that a user would view the pages
- **Hyperlinks view** allows you to organise the links in the web pages
- **Tasks view** provides a grid for inputting tasks you need to complete on your web pages.

Frontpage is one of the many specialist web design packages that can be used to support an end user in developing a website. This next section will provide an overview of Frontpage and some of its key elements that can help in the design of your own multi-page websites.

Following on from the basic screen layout and views, there are a range of options 'Properties' that allow you to set up the layout and format certain features such as the title, colours, margins and language, you can also customise the user and system variables.

In the 'general' tab, the title can be changed. This is the text that will appear across the top of the screen above the browser's menu bar when the page is viewed on the web.

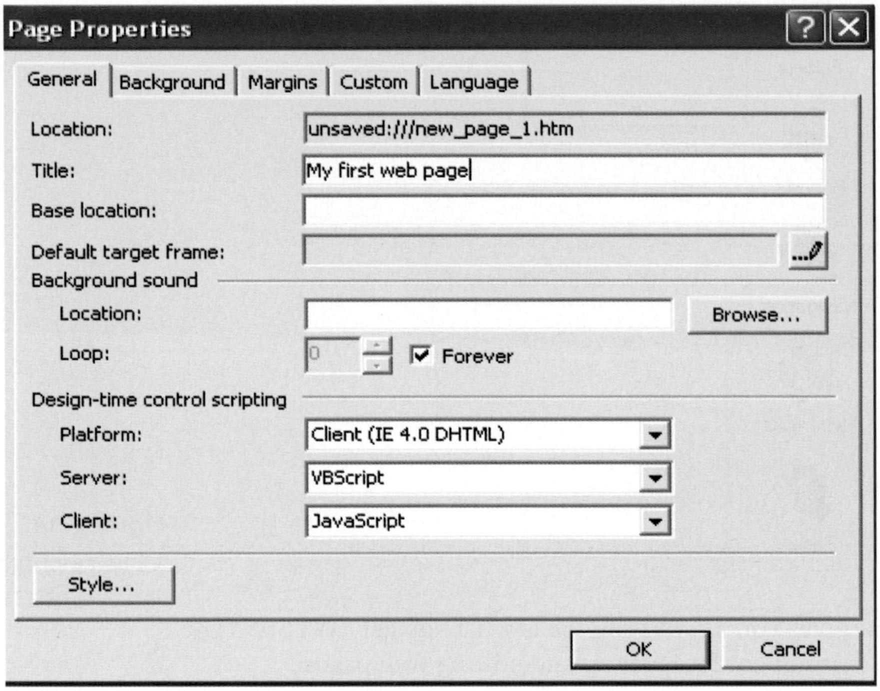

Figure 3.15
Changing the title

The background tab allows you to select and add a background image, change the colour of the text, background and links as shown in Figure 3.16.

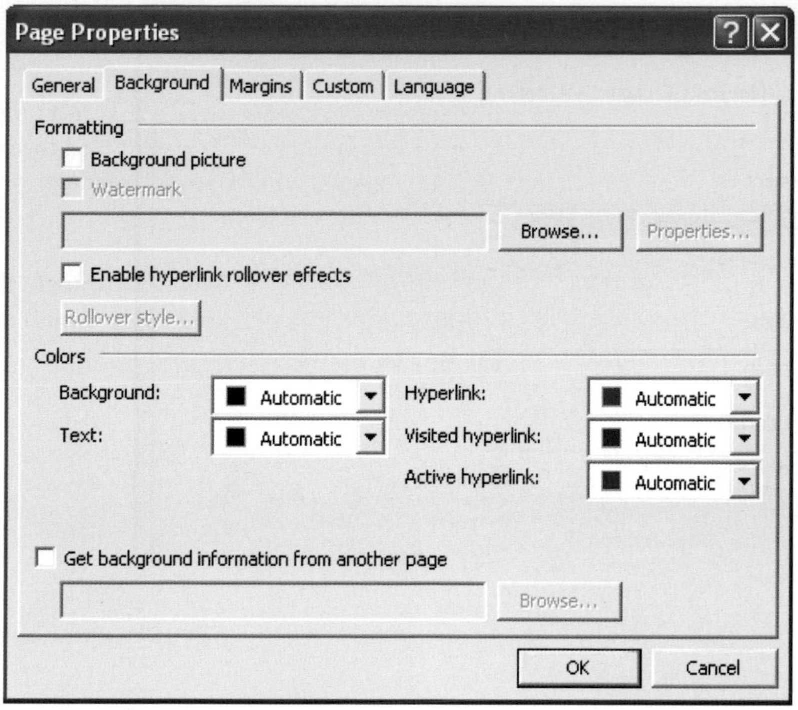

Page Properties ? X

General | Background | Margins | Custom | Language |

Formatting

☐ Background picture
☐ Watermark

[   ] Browse...   Properties...

☐ Enable hyperlink rollover effects

Rollover style...

Colors

Background: ■ Automatic ▼   Hyperlink: ■ Automatic ▼

Text: ■ Automatic ▼   Visited hyperlink: ■ Automatic ▼

Active hyperlink: ■ Automatic ▼

☐ Get background information from another page

[   ] Browse...

OK   Cancel

Figure 3.16
Formatting the
background

The margins can be adjusted, accordingly you can set the top and left
margin width by pixels if necessary.

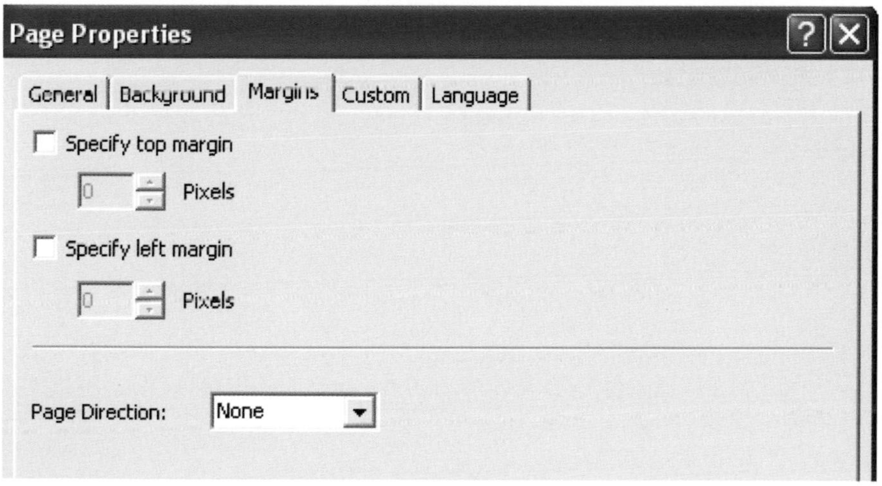

Page Properties ? X

General | Background | Margins | Custom | Language |

☐ Specify top margin

[0 ▲▼] Pixels

☐ Specify left margin

[0 ▲▼] Pixels

Page Direction: [None   ▼]

Figure 3.17
Changing the margins

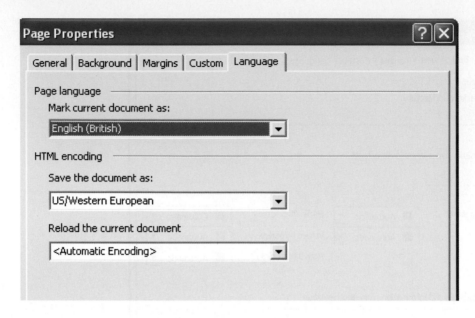

Figure 3.18

Setting the language

The language can also be changed to a specified format as shown in Figure 3.18.

Themes can also be used to customise one or all of the pages to be designed. Themes can be selected and applied – similar to that of Microsoft PowerPoint when designing a presentation.

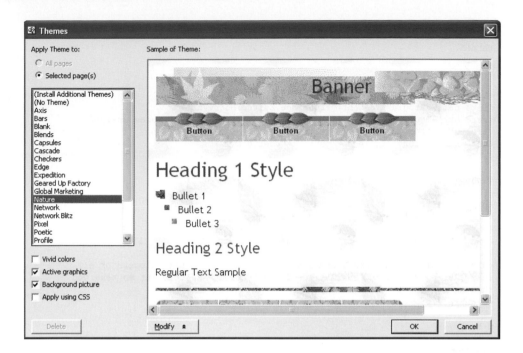

Figure 3.19

Applying a theme

Text

Designing your web pages is very easy in that you can type directly onto the page, apply them and add any graphic as shown in Figure 3.20.

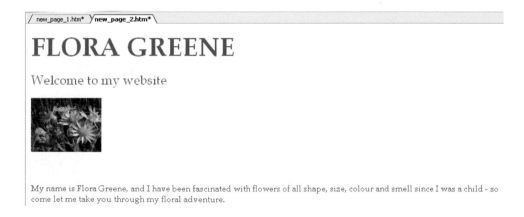

Figure 3.20

Sample website

```
/ new_page_1.htm* \/new_page_2.htm* \
<html>

<head>
<meta http-equiv="Content-Language" content="en-gb">
<meta name="GENERATOR" content="Microsoft FrontPage 5.0">
<meta name="ProgId" content="FrontPage.Editor.Document">
<meta http-equiv="Content-Type" content="text/html; charset=windows-1252">
<title>New Page 2</title>
<meta name="Microsoft Theme" content="poetic 011">
</head>

<body>

<p><font size="7"><b>FLORA GREENE</b></font></p>
<p><font size="5">Welcome to my website</font></p>
<p>
<img border="0" src="file:///C:/Documents/Flowers.jpg" width="133" height="100">
<p> </p>
<p>My name is Flora Greene, and I have been fascinated with flowers of all
shape, size, colour and smell since I was a child - so come let me take you
through my floral adventure.</p>
<p> </p>

</body>

</html>
```

Figure 3.21

HTML view

To view the page in html format this option can simply be selected from the 'view tabs' bar at the bottom of the page as shown in Figure 3.21.

Adding in graphics

Adding in a picture on a web page is really no different to inserting a graphic onto a Microsoft Word document. From the menu bar you just – Insert/Picture/From File and the click on OK.

Activity 2

There are a number of more sophisticated techniques and tools that can be used to make a web page more dynamic. Some of these include:

- Creating a navigation bar
- Hyperlinks
- Frames
- Adding in tables, menus, radio buttons and check boxes, etc.

(a) Based on the information provided set up basic web pages that incorporate different themes, fonts and graphics

(b) Save all progress and then try to explore the software by using some of the more advanced features to further customise the designs that you have created.

Although Frontpage has been used as an example the principles can be carried forward into other web software applications.

Using HTML (Hyper Text Mark-up Language)

Using HTML is very simple in that the content is typed in text and surrounded by certain commands or 'tags'. Tags will be introduced as we go through certain features of a web page.

There are a number of items that you can put onto a web page(s), these include:

- A title
- Headings
- Paragraphs and line breaks
- Lists and menus
- Character formatting
- Links
- Colour

Titles

One of the first items to put on a web page, is a title. The title will appear on the top of every window.

For example, if you wanted a title to be 'My Sample Web Page', you would type:

<title>My Sample Web Page</title>

In HTML, every command is surrounded by '< and >', in most commands you also need to tell the web browser when to end this command. This can be achieved by including a back slash (/) in front of the ending command, as in above.

HTML is not case sensitive therefore <title> is the same as <TITLE>, which is the same as <tITLe>.

Headings

HTML has six levels of headings, numbered 1 through 6, with 1 being the largest and 6 the smallest. Headings are displayed in larger, or smaller fonts, and usually bolder. If you wanted to type 'My website', it would be displayed accordingly as shown in Figure 3.22.

Paragraphs, line breaks and body

Paragraphs can be added by using the following syntax:

<P>This is my sample web page. I will be developing it over the next few weeks. The evidence can be used as part of my assessment</P>

Will result in this:

This is my sample web page. I will be developing it over the next few weeks. The evidence can be used as part of my assessment.

Line breaks   There may be instances where you want to end typing on one line, and start on the next. This can be done by using **
** syntax, and it is one of the few commands that you don't have to put an ending command '/' on. An example of this can be seen with:

**Welcome to my website,
What do you think?
Please leave feedback
My e-mail address is .....**

The result would be

Welcome to my website,
What do you think?
Please leave feedback
My e-mail address is .....

Body

The tag used for identifying a body of text is <body> this is used in conjunction with paragraphs and breaks to clearly identify the content of a section of text.

<h1>My website</h1>

My website

<h2>My website</h2>

My website

<h3>My website</h3>

My website

<h4>My website</h4>

My website

<h5>My website</h5>

My website

<h6>My website</h6>

My website

Figure 3.22

Heading examples in HTML

```
<html>
  <head>
    <title>Test page</title>←————— Would appear in the
                                      title bar at the top
  </head>
  <body>
    <p>My sample web page <p>
    <br>
    <p>What do you think?<p>
  </body>
</html>
```

The sample page would look like this:

My sample web page
What do you think?

Lists and menus

There are two types of lists that you can make in HTML – bulleted and numbered.

To make a bulleted list of: motherboard, hard disk, keyboard, memory, monitor, case, mouse, you would type:

<UL>
<LI> motherboard
<LI> hard disk
<LI> keyboard
<LI> memory
<LI> monitor
<LI> case
<LI> mouse
</UL>

The result being:

- motherboard
- hard disk
- keyboard
- memory
- monitor
- case
- mouse

To make a numbered list of: motherboard, hard disk, keyboard, memory, monitor, case, mouse, you would type:

<OL>
<LI> motherboard
<LI> hard disk
<LI> keyboard
<LI> memory
<LI> monitor
<LI> case
<LI> mouse
</OL>

The result being:

1. motherboard
2. hard disk
3. keyboard
4. memory
5. monitor
6. case
7. mouse

Menus

Menus give the end user an option of selecting items from a list without having to type information in. Two types of menus that can be used include a 'pull-down' menu and a 'scroll' menu. On a pull-down menu, if you wanted to find out the best background colour to use for a web page you could use the 'selected' command to have an initial default option and then list other colours so a user could choose a colour other than black, if preferred.

What is your preferred background for a web page?
<SELECT NAME="colour">
<OPTION>Red
<OPTION>Yellow   Preferred option
<OPTION>Orange
<OPTION>Green
<OPTION>Blue
<OPTION>Purple
<OPTION SELECTED>Black
<OPTION>Brown
</SELECT> <P>

The result would be:

What is your preferred background for a web page?

However, more colour options would be available once you clicked on the arrow of the pull-down menu.

With a scroll-down menu you can give the end user an option of selecting more than one item. This can be done by holding down the 'command' or 'shift key' and then clicking on the items.

If a question was posed: 'What is your favourite games console? With the answers being XBox 360, Sony Playstation 2 or Nintendo Gamecube, the text that you would type for each list is:

What is your favourite video games console?
<SELECT NAME="video game" SIZE=3>
<OPTION VALUE="Xbox 360">Xbox 360
<OPTION VALUE="PS2">Sony Playstation 2
<OPTION VALUE="Gamecube">Nintendo Gamecube
</SELECT><P>

The result would be:

What is your favourite games console?

An example of how drop-down menus work can be shown in Figure 3.23 with the Elsevier website (www.elsevier.com) and source code.

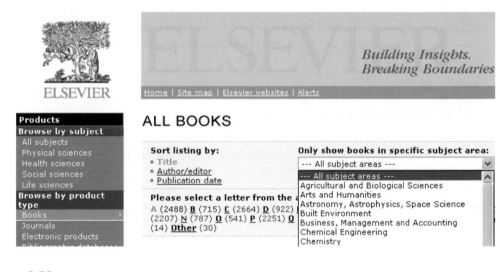

Figure 3.23

Example of a drop-down menu

```
<tr>
<td class="verdana11DarkGrey"><b>Only show books in specific subject
area:</b></td>
</tr>

<tr>
<td><img src="/authored_framework/images/empty.gif" width="1" height="3"
border="0" alt="" /></td>
</tr>

<tr>
<td>
<select name="subject" size="1" class="locationSelect"
onchange="window.location.href=document.subjectSelect.subject[document.subjectS
elect.subject.selectedIndex].value">

<option
value="/wps/find/books_browse.cws_home?pseudotype=&sortBy=Title&letter=A"
selected>  ---  All subject areas  ---</option>

<option
value="/wps/find/books_browse.cws_home/L01?pseudotype=&sortBy=Title&SH1Co
de=L01&letter=A">Agricultural and Biological Sciences</option>

<option
value="/wps/find/books_browse.cws_home/S01?pseudotype=&sortBy=Title&SH1Co
de=S01&letter=A">Arts and Humanities</option>

<option
value="/wps/find/books_browse.cws_home/P01?pseudotype=&sortBy=Title&SH1Co
de=P01&letter=A">Astronomy, Astrophysics, Space Science</option>

<option
value="/wps/find/books_browse.cws_home/P02?pseudotype=&sortBy=Title&SH1Co
de=P02&letter=A">Built Environment</option>

<option
value="/wps/find/books_browse.cws_home/S02?pseudotype=&sortBy=Title&SH1Co
de=S02&letter=A">Business, Management and Accounting</option>

<option
value="/wps/find/books_browse.cws_home/P03?pseudotype=&sortBy=Title&SH1Co
de=P03&letter=A">Chemical Engineering</option>

<option
value="/wps/find/books_browse.cws_home/P04?pseudotype=&sortBy=Title&SH1Co
de=P04&letter=A">Chemistry</option>
```

Figure 3.24

Elsevier example of drop down menu and source code

Character formatting

At some stage you may want to change the format of your text using a range of 'text styles'. There are a number of styles that can be used which include:

\<i\>, \</i\> for *italic*
\<b\>, \</b\> for **bold**
\<u\>, \</u\> for <u>underlined</u>
\<strike\>, \</strike\> for ~~strikeout~~
\<sup\>, \</sup\> for superscript
\<sub\>, \</sub\> for subscript
\<tt\>, \</tt\> for `teletype`
\<blink\>, \</blink\> for blinking text

Links

Links can be identified by coloured text or graphic that takes you to another location when you click over them. A link takes you to another area of the same page or to another website.

If for example, you wanted to make a link from your web page to The Training and Education Company, the URL being:

http://www.train-ed.co.uk

you would enter:

\<A HREF="http://www.train-ed.co.uk"\>Whatever text that you want to be coloured would be placed here\</A\>

The result would be:

<u>What ever text that you want to be coloured would be placed here</u>

Some people have a link on their web page that will automatically send an e-mail to a certain address. To do this, if you wanted people to recognise that you had a support e-mail facility, your e-mail address was abc@123.co.uk, you could type:

\<A HREF="mailto:abc@123.co.uk"\>Support\</a\>

The result being:

Support

Colour

Colour is required in a number of areas on a web page to capture the users' attention, direct users to a specific area and promote the product or service being advertised. Colour can be applied to the background, main text, visited, non-visited and active links by using the syntax as shown:

- <body bgcolour="#code"> for background colour
- <body text="#code"> for colour of text (non-hyperlinked items)
- <body link="#code"> for colour of unvisited links
- <body vlink="#code"> for colour of visited links
- <body alink="#code"> for colour of active links (during selection).

The colour codes available to use are quite extensive, and can be selected by name, or by 'hex' code a sample of which can be seen in Figure 3.25.

Hex Code	Color	Hex Code	Color	Hex Code	Color
#66FFFF		#33FFFF		#00FFFF	
#66FFCC		#33FFCC		#00FFCC	
#66FF99		#33FF99		#00FF99	
#66FF66		#33FF66		#00FF66	
#66FF33		#33FF33		#00FF33	
#66FF00		#33FF00		#00FF00	
#66CCFF		#33CCFF		#00CCFF	
#66CCCC		#33CCCC		#00CCCC	
#66CC99		#33CC99		#00CC99	
#66CC66		#33CC66		#00CC66	
#66CC33		#33CC33		#00CC33	
#66CC00		#33CC00		#00CC00	
#6699FF		#3399FF		#0099FF	
#6699CC		#3399CC		#0099CC	
#669999		#339999		#009999	
#669966		#339966		#009966	
#669933		#339933		#009933	
#669900		#339900		#009900	

Figure 3.25
Hex colour codes

Activity 3

(a) Design a basic web page(s) using HTML
(b) Incorporate a range of features as discussed throughout this section to include:
  • headings
  • lists
  • paragraphed text
  • colour
  (more advanced features that incorporate links and menu items can also be included)
(c) Show that you have thought about the design by presenting draft copies of the pages(s) prior to the physical design.

On-line software

Another option to designing a website is to outsource to another company but still have input into the actual design in terms of layout and aesthetics. This option is very desirable for people that do not have the time or skills to embark on using specialist software or HTML.

Embedded software

Embedded software such as Macromedia Flash can be used in conjunction with HTML. Flash adds the dynamic element by allowing text, images and animations to move around on the screen.

Reviewing and checking websites

Once you have selected the software or organisation to design your website, you need to ensure that it meets the original requirements in terms of who it is aimed at and its function.

In addition the final website should be checked to ensure that:

(1) the colours are appropriate
(2) the layout is clear and aesthetically pleasing
(3) all links are working
(4) it is easy to navigate through
(5) the content is correct, current and appropriate for its target audience
(6) all graphics and animation enhance the website
(7) the site downloads quickly and easily.

In terms of publishing the website, again a number of steps need to be taken to ensure that the files are uploaded onto an Intranet, Internet, FTP or local server. Once the website is 'live' you also need to make sure that the content is maintained and updated regularly, that file management procedures are applied in terms of naming, moving and deleting files.

Finally registration with a range of search engines will ensure that your site will have a greater opportunity of being accessed by the public.

Chapter 4

Networking essentials

This chapter will enable students to gain an insight into the uses, role and application of networks in organisations. Networks can bring a range of benefits to the way in which users communicate and share information. In conjunction, there are a number of issues that surround the use of networks that include security, and data protection; this unit will address a range of these concerns.

The expectations of the 'networking essentials' unit is that you will be involved with a range of practical activities on a small scale. To support this, the chapter will provide a good coverage of network basics, topologies, features, services, connectivity issues, hardware and software.

This chapter will allow students to gain a good understanding of network functions and the types of networks that are used in organisations. In addition, students will also be able to understand the features and services of both local and wide area network technologies. Finally, students will be provided with information on hardware and software and how they are connected and configured to support any practical tasks that may be required as part of the unit assessment.

When you complete this unit you should be able to:

(1) Understand the use of computer networks
(2) Understand the features and services of local and wide area network technologies
(3) Understand network hardware and software components and how they are connected and configured
(4) Be able to set up and use a simple local area network.

Understand the use of computer networks

Networks and communication

Networks can indeed enhance and benefit communication systems within organisations. Information can be exchanged on an individual-to-individual need, team need or a functional need internally within an organisation as shown in Figure 4.1.

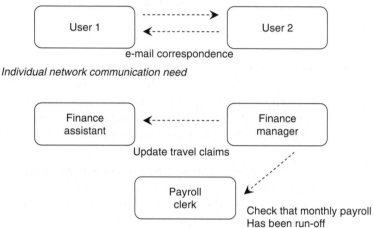

Individual network communication need

Finance – Team based network communication need

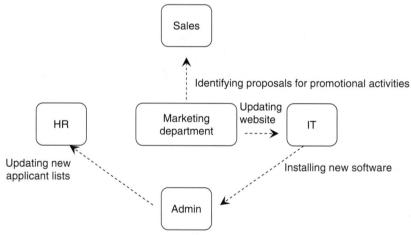

Functional network communication need

Figure 4.1

Example network information exchange

In addition, networks can enhance communication outside of the organisation to extend to offering support to customers, ordering items from suppliers (online) and submitting financial returns and documents to third parties.

Networks can also be used for research purposes – use of the Internet, as an information resource and to provide a framework for standard ways of working in terms of coordinating tasks, collaboration, informing, updating and disseminating data and information to a range of sources.

The effective use of a network does however mean that it is not just a simple task of connecting up and using the resource. Networks are supported by a wide variety of resources that all need to be managed effectively to ensure optimal usage and compliance. Some of these include:

Managing network resources

- information
- hardware
- software
- people – staffing, users, etc.
- administration (compliance with legislation, auditing, network policies and procedures).

A network is only as effective as the resources used to support and manage it.

Information

Information is required to determine the initial need and function of the network – what purpose will it serve? Will it increase efficiency? Will it improve communication? Will it save the company money in the future? Information needs to be captured initially to address the feasibility of having a network. Information is also required at every stage of the implementation. How will the network fit in with existing systems and platforms? What users/departments will have access? How will it be utilised? Finally information will be needed to allow effective monitoring of the network and day-to-day use to assess its performance against original targets etc. Is the network meeting up to its expectations?

Hardware and software

Hardware and software, the actual mechanics of the network need to be addressed very carefully, as these resources are very expensive, especially if something goes wrong. Considerations need to be given as to how a network will be integrated with any other existing systems. Will there be any conflicts or compatibility issues across different systems and platforms?

Different network types will also be hardware- and software-dependent; will the network be cable or wireless for example? Does the network have to support 10 or 1,000 user?

Is the network confined to a single department or branches across the country? All of these considerations will impact upon the hardware and software to be used.

People – staffing

People/end users/administrators all play an important role in a networking environment. There are a number of issues concerning the management of this resource. Initially users need to be considered when a network is being implemented within an organisation in terms of how will a network impact upon their working environment? Will the networked environment be easy for users to understand, or will training be required? Who will look after the network and ensure that it remains secure and monitored regularly? In terms of additional staffing, a networked environment may require technical support personnel and administrators to ensure that the network operates at an optimum level on a day-to-day basis.

Administration

Working within a networked environment can raise some issues about how data is captured, stored and shared across users and at an organisational level. With any amount of users at any one time having access to shared, possibly sensitive information regarding customers, students, patients or clients, an organisation needs to demonstrate that they are working within the framework of certain legislation. Legislation such as the Data Protection Act 1998 offers protection to third parties and ensures that organisations and end users are compliant.

Disadvantages of networks

Networks do indeed offer a whole host of benefits as previously explored, however there are some drawbacks to working within a shared environment as shown in Figure 4.2.

Ensuring that you have the right network installed to meet the demands of your organisations and the growing needs of end users is paramount. If a network has been installed that is not robust enough to

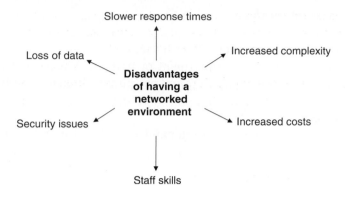

Figure 4.2
Disadvantages of
networks

cope with the amount of users connected, then the response times will be slower. In addition if there is inadequate storage to accommodate users on the network, data will be at risk of not being backed-up.

The complexity and costs associated with a networked environment can spiral depending upon the function of the network, number of users and physical location.

Staff skills may need to be addressed because end users could require training, new staff members may also have to be recruited to offer technical network support.

Security of networks is paramount to ensure that data stored is not corrupted, infected, destroyed or sabotaged either internally or externally. In addition, the loss of data could cost an organisation hundreds, thousands or even greater amounts financially and reputably.

Network features

Networks vary in size and complexity, some are used in a single department or office and others extend across local, national or international branches. Networks vary in structure to accommodate the need to exchange information across short or wide geographical areas. These structures include:

* local area networks (LAN)
* metropolitan area network (MAN)
* wide area networks (WAN) – long haulage networks (LHN)
* value added networks (VAN).

Features and services of local and wide area network technologies

Local area networks

These consist of computers that located physically close to each other – within the same department or branch. A typical structure would include a set of computers and peripherals linked as individual nodes.

Each node, for example a computer and shared peripheral, is directly connected by cables that serve as a pathway for transferring data between machines.

Metropolitan area networks

These are more efficient than a LAN and use fibre optic cables to allow more information and a higher complexity of information. The range of a MAN is also greater than a LAN allowing business to expand – however, this can prove to be expensive because of the fibre optic cabling.

Wide area networks – long haulage networks

These are networks that extend over a larger geographical distance from city to city within the same country or across countries and even continents. WANs transfer data between LANs on a backbone system using digital, satellite or even microwave technology. A WAN will connect different servers at a site, when this connection is from a PC on one site to a server on another it is referred to as being 'remote'. If this coverage is international, it is referred to as being an 'enterprise-wide network'.

Value added network

This type of network is a data network that has all the benefits of a WAN but with vastly reduced costs. The cost of setting up and maintaining this type of network is reduced because the service provider rents out the network to different companies as opposed to an organisation having sole ownership or 'point-to-point' private line.

Networks can be used to support a range of applications within an organisation, the selection of a particular network depends upon:

(i)   the application/use
(ii) number of users requiring access

(iii) physical resources
(iv) scope of the network – within a room, department, across departments or branches.

If, for example, a network was required to link a few computers within the same department to enable the sharing of certain resources, a LAN might be installed.

If, however, a network was required to link branches and supplier sources across the country, a WAN might be installed with the server located at the Head Office providing remote access to users connecting at individual branches.

Test your knowledge

(1) What is meant by LAN, WAN and MAN?
(2) Why does a WAN differ from a LAN?
(3) Why is a value added network better than a WAN?
(4) What type of network might you consider if you wanted to link four computers together in a single office?

Network topologies

There are a number of different network topologies (topology referring to the layout of connected devices on a network) these include:

- Bus
- Ring
- Star
- Tree
- Mesh

A bus topology is based on a single cable which forms the backbone to the structure with devices that are attached to the cable through an 'interface connector' as shown in Figure 4.3. When a device needs to communicate with another device on the network a message is broadcast. Although only the intended receiving device can accept and process the message, a disadvantage of this topology is the fact that other devices on the network can also see the message.

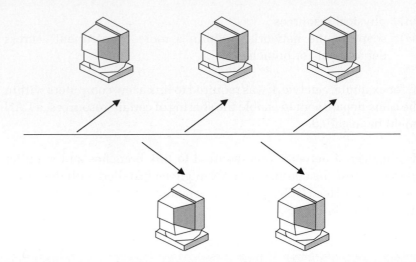

Figure 4.3
Bus topology

In a ring topology, every device has two neighbours for communication purposes as shown in Figure 4.4. Communication travels in one direction only either clockwise or anticlockwise.

One disadvantage of this type of topology is that a failure in the cable can disable the entire network.

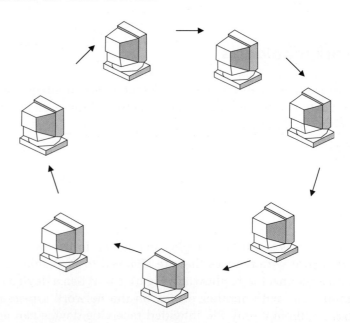

Figure 4.4
Ring topology

Star topologies are based around a central connection point referred to as a 'hub' or a 'switch' as shown in Figure 4.5. A series of cables are used in this type of network that gives the advantage that if one cable fails only one computer will go down and the remainder of

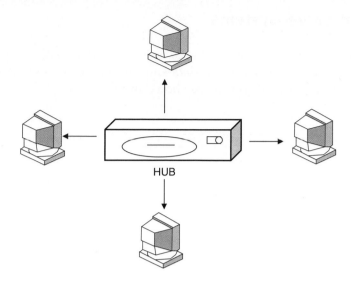

Figure 4.5
Star topology

the network will remain active. If the hub fails, however, the entire network will fail.

Tree topologies integrate a number of star topologies together onto a bus – with the hub devices connecting directly to the tree bus, each hub acting as the 'root' of the tree device.

A mesh topology introduces the concept of 'routes', where several messages can be sent on the network via several possible pathways from source to destination.

Activity 1

Produce a table comparing each of the type of network topologies discussed.

Use the points below as guidance of areas to compare:

- Direction of data travel
- Robustness – what happens if a cable fails?
- Speed – you may have to think about this one based on the information provided.

Client/server systems

The client/server approach is based around a client that is responsible for processing requests for data and the server that executes the request and returns its results as shown in Figure 4.6.

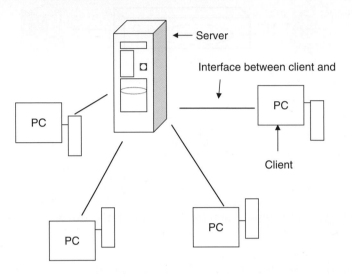

Figure 4.6

Example of a client/server

The client element requires 'intelligence' (e.g. memory) therefore, most clients are PCs, a 'dumb' terminal will not work because it lacks memory. The PCs are access points for end-user applications.

The server is a more powerful computer that stores the application and the data that is shared by users. They effectively circulate the information around the network and together with the network operating system, perform a number of functions as shown in Figure 4.7.

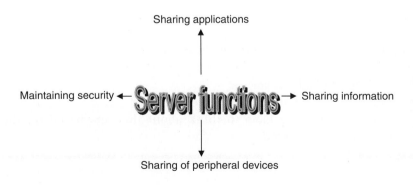

Figure 4.7

Server functions

Applications and data can be managed more effectively when they are managed by a server. Auditing functions can also be undertaken more easily to ensure that data is being kept secure.

All of the machines on the Internet are either servers or clients. The machines that provide services to other machines are servers. And the machines that are used to connect to those services are clients. Servers can be categorised into the following:

- web servers
- print servers
- e-mail servers
- file transfer protocol (FTP) servers
- newsgroup servers
- storage servers

When you connect to a website to read a page, you are accessing that sites web server.

Peer-to-peer networking

Peer-to-peer (P2P) networking does not use a client and server framework but operates through a system of 'peer nodes' that functions as both the client and server simultaneously. As a result, P2P networking holds many advantages over a client/server system to include:

- shared resources of P2P networking can be directly accessed
- more reliable because it has a network of 'peers' as opposed to a single server that could fail at any time
- resources on a P2P network can be shared centrally or on the edge of the network, in oppose to a client/server framework where resources can only be accessed centrally.

One of the more famous examples of information sharing using a P2P network can be seen in the growth of the music sharing service 'Napster' as shown in Figure 4.8.

Figure 4.8

Napster

Source: Napster.co.uk

Activity 2

(a) Carry out research on how 'Napster' originated and who the founder was. Identify what happened to 'Napster' and why it has now been taken over

(b) Produce an A4 information leaflet or a 6-page presentation slide based on your findings.

Network access methods

In networking, you need to access a resource in order to use it. Access methods are the rules that define how a computer puts data onto a computer cable and takes it off. Once data is flowing across the network, the access method regulates this flow of traffic. There are a number of ways in which resources can be accessed, these include:

- Carrier-sense-multiple-access $\Big\langle$ with collision detection (CD)
  with collision avoidance (CA)
- Token passing
- Demand priority

Carrier-sense multiple access with collision detection checks the cable for each computer on the network for 'network traffic'. As soon as a computer senses that the cable is traffic-free, it can send its data. Once this has been transmitted, no other computer can send data until the original data has reached its destination and the cable then becomes free again.

A data collision will occur if two or more computers decide to send data simultaneously, when this happens the computers that are attempting this data transmission will need to stop and then after a period of time try to re-transmit. The period of wait is determined by each computer involved, thus reducing the chance of another collision caused by simultaneous data sends.

Carrier-sense multiple access with collision avoidance is a method whereby each computer signals when it is about to transmit data, prior to sending. With this method, other computers will know if a collision might happen and so therefore will wait until the cable is free from traffic.

Token passing uses a special packet called a 'token' that circulates around a cable ring passing from computer to computer. In order for a computer to send data across the network it must wait for a free token. When the token is detected by the computer and it has control of it, it will be able to send the data.

This access method known as demand priority is designed for the 100-Mbps Ethernet standard known as 100VG-AnyLAN. It is based on the notion that repeaters and end nodes are the two components that make up all 100VG-AnyLAN networks. The repeaters manage the network access by doing round-robin searches for requests to send from all nodes on the network. The repeater, or hub, is responsible for noting all links, addresses and end nodes and checking that they are all working accordingly.

What does this mean?

End node – can be a computer, router, bridge or switch.

Test your knowledge

(1) What is meant by a network topology?

(2) Identify three types of topologies and give a brief overview as to how they work?

(3) What do the following terminologies mean:
  • Client/server
  • Peer-to-peer
  • Access method

(4) Identify three types of access methods.

Network services

There are a number of services that can be provided in a network environment. Users can be linked together to:

• Share data and information and disseminate good practice across an organisation
• Increase efficiency
• Enable the sharing of resources e.g. printers and scanners
• Reduce information transfer time
• Reduce costs.

As a result of these services and subsequent benefits, many organisations opt for a networked solution despite the initial financial outlay, set-up costs, possible disruption to employees, the need to train and update.

Networks have enabled organisations to address a range of business solutions through the use of different types of software applications and communication tools, more specifically the growth in 'groupware' tools such as:

  (i)   e-mail
  (ii) voicemail
  (iii) teleconferencing and videoconferencing
  (iv) facsimile (fax servers for desktop fax)
  (v)   collaboration/workgroup software

and the setting up of intranets, extranets, bulleting boards, newsgroups and the use of the Internet have enabled organisations to become more competitive and more flexible in their business practices.

Service types

There are a number of services available over a network such as:

- Communication services – e-mail, conferencing
- File transfer
- Interaction and integration with other software, such as databases.

Communication services

E-mail is the transmission of a message or messages across a communication network. The popularity of e-mail has risen due to the speed of which messages can be transmitted, the ability to share data and send multiple copies. Other advantages of e-mail include the cost in relation to using other communication mediums, the ability to attach a range of multimedia to text documents (pictures, movie clips, hyperlinks, etc.) and auditing – users can store messages (sent and received), track documents by date, time and author and also generate receipts.

Voicemail provides users with the option of setting up a recorded message to capture information that may have been lost if the recipient of the information was not available to take a call.

Conferencing applications range from text, white boarding and more commonly video conferencing. Conferencing facilities allow users to communicate interactively over a set distance.

Facsimile transmits an image through a telephone connection. Faxes can be sent through a conventional fax machine or through a fax modem.

Collaboration software provides the opportunity for groups of users to interact within a secure environment. Collaboration could take the form of an on-line discussion, verbal communication via a microphone or active participation in the creation or editing of documentation.

File transfer

File transfer is used to transmit any type of file (program, text, graphic, multimedia file, etc.) using a process that bunches the data into packets. When the package of data arrives at its destination, the receiving system/computer checks it to make sure that no errors have been picked up during transmission and then returns a message to confirm receipt of the package and instructions that it is ready to receive another packet as shown in Figure 4.9.

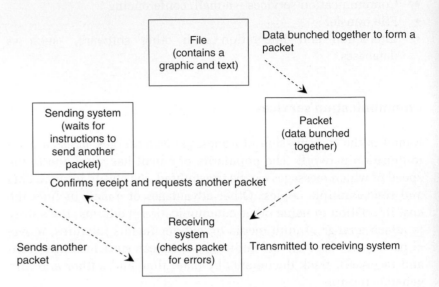

Figure 4.9

File transfer process

Integration and interaction with other software

Distributed databases   A major advantage of an organisation using a network rather than a series of stand-alone computers is that users can all access the same database. This is extremely important in environments where data is continually being edited and updated. Interacting with databases is an essential part of 'electronic data interchange' (EDI), a network service that automatically exchanges data.

Distributed databases consist of two or more data files, each located in different areas on a network. As a result, different users can get access to the data sets without disrupting other users.

The use of a distributed database system can create a number of issues, some of these are positive and others negative.

The positive issues or advantages of using a distributed database include:

(i)   Reliability and availability: because of the distributed element if one part of the database crashes or fails it will not disable the entire database, other data sets in other areas can still be accessed

(ii) Autonomy of data: users at one site can have control over their own data

(iii) Growth/expansion: this type of system can be expanded to incorporate more data sets in other areas of the network.

The negative issues/disadvantages of using a distributed database include:

(i) Cost: in terms of set-up charges, installation, hardware and software

(ii) Complexity: setting up a distributed database, ensuring that all data sets can be accessed

(iii) Security: controlling and monitoring the network and data control issues.

Although there are many advantages, there are also some disadvantages with distributed databases as illustrated in the case study 'Distributed databases, distributed headaches'. The case study outlines some of the many disadvantages with distributed databases and the way forward for distributed computing.

Case study

DATAMATION®   ⦁EARTHWEB

Distributed databases, distributed headaches

By Karen D. Schwartz

Chuck Shellhouse knows really big databases. Shellhouse, the Colorado Springs-based director of service operations in the information technology division of MCI, is responsible for managing more than 40 terabytes of data located in datacenters around the country. Those databases, which primarily run DB2 and Adabas on IBM and Hitachi mainframes, contain all of the business applications needed to run the telecommunications company's entire $20+ billion revenue stream.

Even though MCI's database dwarfs the databases of most corporations, MCI's computing model has become increasingly common. With companies generating and keeping more data to make better decisions on how to make money, many organizations now rely on the model of geographically dispersed, multiterabyte databases.

But today's forward-thinking companies are changing the definition of distributed computing. No longer are they managing hundreds of distributed environments running small servers. By and large, they've found such set-ups, which involve installing software and backing up data at each location, to be time-consuming and expensive.

Instead, these companies have consolidated their data into just a few datacenters, housing

"In a typical data center in the old days, the technical-support people could see and touch the hardware. That isn't the case anymore," says Chuck Shellhouse, MCI's director of service operations, IT division.
Photo: Steve Starr/SABA

much larger amounts of data at each center. At MCI, Shellhouse and his staff used to manage numerous datacenters in many locations around the country. But with managerial problems and costs spiraling — the datacenters required on-site support personnel, operational personnel, and systems programmers at each location — Shellhouse and his team devised a plan to replace those datacenters with 'megacenters' on the backbone of MCI's network. Today, the company has just four datacenters.

Consolidating a dozen datacenters into a few makes a lot of sense for most large companies, says Daniel Graham, a Somers, N.Y.-based strategy and operations executive in IBM's Global Business Intelligence Solutions group.

'Having [distributed datacenters] is like having children. Two are wonderful, four are a lot of fun, six start to be a drain on your resources, and 20 are impossible', Graham says. 'Every time you have another child, you have bought yourself a certain amount of overhead cost'.

The Internet: a new paradigm

Database experts have seen the future of distributed computing, and it is the Internet. The Internet provides IT managers with an easier mechanism for distributing data to end users. By simplifying and consolidating on one universal client, they can contact their customers and work with their business partners much more easily.

The Internet changes the whole paradigm of distributed computing, says Carl Olofson, research director for database management systems at International Data Corp., the Framingham, Mass., consulting firm.

'Ultimately, instead of an organization having a fixed topology of networks that have to be connected together, they can employ a much more flexible scheme using the Internet instead of allowing regional offices to connect through their system', Olofson says. In addition, the Internet enables companies to connect to each other and create virtual enterprises, he notes.

http://www.itmanagement.earthweb.com

Case study review questions

(1) Identify the problems that MCI encountered by consolidating their data into datacentres
(2) How did MCI address these problems?
(3) What role does the Internet play in terms of distributed computing?

Distributed database systems also allows applications to be accessed from local and remote databases. The two types of system include:

*   Homogenous distributed database system
*   Heterogeneous distributed database system

Within a homogenous distributed database system, the network consists of two or more Oracle databases that exist on one or more machines. An application can therefore simultaneously access or modify the data in several databases as shown in Figure 4.10 illustrating four databases and their related clients. The underlying technology to support this is referred to as 'clustering'. Homogeneous databases all use the same database management system (DBMS) software and have the same applications on each computer.

In a heterogeneous distributed database system, the architecture is the same as shown in Figure 4.10, however, at least one of the databases is non-Oracle. Heterogeneous databases have a high degree of local autonomy, each computer has its own local users, applications and data and only connects to other computers on the network for the

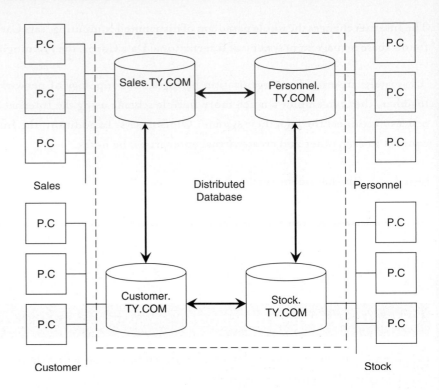

Figure 4.10

Example of a distributed system

information that it does not have. This type of distributed database is also referred to as a 'federated system'.

Protocols

Communication between different devices need to agree on the format of the data. The set of rules that define the format is known as a 'protocol'. A communications protocol therefore provides a set of rules to define data representation, error detection, signalling and authentication.

An effective communications protocol must define the following in terms of transmission:

* the rate (in bauds or bps)
* synchronous or asynchronous
* full-duplex or half-duplex mode

Protocols can be incorporated in either the hardware or the software and they are arranged in a layered format (sometimes referred to as a protocol stack) as shown in Figure 4.11. They provide some or all of the services specified by a layer in the Open Systems Interconnection (OSI) model.

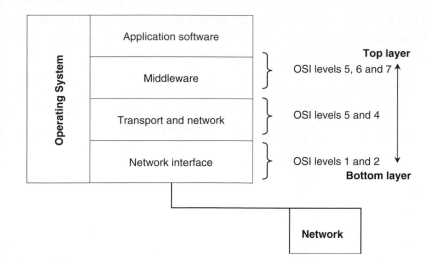

Figure 4.11
Protocol layers

The OSI layer model

When setting up a network correctly, you need to be aware of the major standards organisations and how their work can affect network communications. In 1984, the International Organisation for Standardisation (ISO) released the OSI reference model which has subsequently become an international standard and serves as a guide for networking procedures and visualising networking environments.

The model provides a description of how network hardware and software can work together in a layered framework to promote communications. The model also provides a frame of how components are supposed to function which assists with troubleshooting problems.

The OSI reference model divides network communication into seven layers. Each layer covers different network activities, equipment or protocols as shown in the table below.

Levels	Description
7	Applications layer
6	Presentation layer
5	Session layer
4	Transport layer
3	Network layer
2	Data link layer
1	Physical layer

Physical layer: provides the interface between the medium and the device. The layer transmits bits and defines how the data is transmitted over the network. It also defines what control signals are used and the physical network properties such as cable size, connector, etc.

Data link layer: provides functional, procedural and error detection and correction facilities between network entities.

Network layer: provides packing routing facilities across a network.

Transport layer: an intermediate layer that higher layers use to communicate to the network layer.

Session layer: the interface between a user and the network, this layer keeps communication flowing.

Presentation layer: ensures that the same language is being spoken by computers, for example converting text to ASCII and encoding and decoding binary data.

Applications layer: ensures that the programs being accessed directly by a user can communicate, e.g. an e-mail program.

Transmission control protocol/Internet protocol (TCP/IP)

TCP/IP is the standard protocol used for communication amongst different systems. TCP/IP also supports routing and is commonly used as an Internet-working protocol.

Other protocols written specifically for the TCP/IP suite include:

- File Transfer Protocol (FTP) for exchanging files amongst computers that use TCP/IP
- Simple Mail Transfer Protocol (SMTP) for e-mail
- Simple Network Management Protocol (SNMP) for network management.

There are many advantages of TCP/IP including:

(1) Expandability – because it uses scalable cross-platform client/server architecture and it can expand to accommodate future needs
(2) Industry standard – being an open protocol means that it is not managed/controlled by a single company, therefore it is less prone to compatibility issues. It is the de facto protocol of the Internet
(3) Versatility – it contains a set of utilities for connecting different operating systems, therefore connectivity is not dependent on the network operating system used on either computer.

Test your knowledge

(1) What is meant by a 'protocol'?
(2) What do the following stand for:
 - OSI
 - FTP
 - SMTP
 - TCP/IP
 - SNMP
(3) How many layers are there in the OSI model and what are they?
(4) Give one advantage of TCP/IP.

Data security issues

Although networks can bring many benefits to an organisation, there are also some drawbacks to having a networked environment. One of the major drawbacks is caused by the 'shared' element of using a network and the increased security risks.

The security risks can be categorised into:

- unauthorised access by internal users and external threats
- vandalism, theft and sabotage.

Keeping data secure on a network can be quite difficult because of the environment in which users work and levels of user and access requirements to the data. With the movement towards a totally networked environment promoting a culture of 'sharing' the issue of data security is even more important and should be addressed at a number of levels. Measures that can be taken to protect network traffic against illegal access and other security threats can be seen in Figure 4.12.

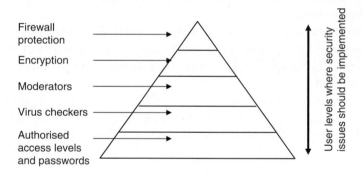

Figure 4.12

Security measures

Firewall protection

The primary aim of a firewall is to guard against unauthorised access to an internal network. In effect, a firewall is a gateway with a lock, the gateway only opens for information packets that pass one or more security inspections.

There are three basic types of firewalls, these include:

(i) Application gateways – the first gateways sometimes referred to as proxy gateways. These are made up of hosts that run special software to act as a proxy server. Clients behind the firewall must know how to use the proxy, and be configured to do so in order to use Internet services. This software runs at the 'application layer' of the ISO/OSI Reference Model, hence the name. Traditionally application gateways have been the most secure, because they don't allow anything to pass by default, but need to have the programs written and turned on in order to begin passing traffic

(ii) Packet filtering – is a technique whereby routers have 'access control lists' turned on. By default, a router will pass all traffic sent it, and will do so without any sort of restrictions. Access control is performed at a lower ISO/OSI layer (typically, the transport or session layer). Due to the fact that packet filtering is done with routers, it is often much faster than application gateways

(iii) Hybrid system – a mixture between application gateways and packet filtering. In some of these systems, new connections must be authenticated and approved at the application layer. Once this has been done, the remainder of the connection is passed down to the session layer, where packet filters observe the connection to ensure that only packets that are part of an ongoing (already authenticated and approved) conversation are being passed.

Encryption and filtering software

Encryption software scrambles message transmissions – when a message is encrypted a secret numerical code is applied 'encryption key', the message can be transmitted or stored in indecipherable characters. The message can only be read after it has been reconstructed through the use of a 'matching key'.

Moderators

Moderators have the responsibility of controlling, filtering and restricting information that gets shared across a network.

Virus checkers

These programs are designed to search for viruses, notify users of their existence and remove them from infected files or disks.

VeriSign are used by a multitude of organisation both large and small, their ability to provide tailored network security solutions can be seen in their portfolio of customer profiles.

Overall there are a number of data security issues that can impact upon users of all types. At an organisational level, this is more intense because of the number of users that have access to data and the greater risk from external threats. There are a range of measures that can be used to address these threats that fall into internal and external measures as explored earlier, an overview of which is provided in Table 4.1.

Table 4.1

Internal and external security measures

Internal	External
Passwords	Legislation e.g.
Encryption	
Filtering and monitoring software	• Data Protection Act (1984 and 1988)
Employ a moderator/s	• Computer Misuse Act (1990)
Virus checkers and protectors	
Internal security policies and generate an awareness of do's and don'ts	
User access levels	
Firewall	

Test your knowledge

(1) What security risks exist on a networked system and what measures can be taken to address these?
(2) There are three different types of firewall, explain what each firewall type listed is and how it works?
   – Application gateways
   – Packet filtering
   – Hybrid systems
(3) What does encryption do?
(4) Why should audit control measures be used in an organisation?

The consequences of an organisation losing data can be very severe and the disruption to processing activities is costly and time consuming. Attempts to retrieve lost data (if retrievable) can prove to be a fruitless exercise putting strain on a both manual and financial resources.

There are a number of backup options available to an organisation these include:

- Simple backup
- Stack backup
- Advanced stack backup
- Incremental backup
- Grandfather, father, son backup

Simple backup is the elementary backup type. Each time an archive is created, the oldest version of the backup file is replaced with the newly created one.

Stack backup consists of the last created backup and previous versions – the previous versions being organised into a stack format.

The advanced backup procedure differs in that it does not permit unchanged or unedited files in the old backup version copies to be stacked.

An incremental backup provides a fast method of backing up data much faster than a full backup. During an incremental backup, only the files that have changed since the last full or incremental backup are included, as a result the time it takes to conduct the backup may be a fraction of the time it takes to perform a full backup.

The grandfather, father, son backup technique is probably the most common backup method that uses a rotation set of backup disks or tapes, so that three different versions of the same data are held at any one time. An example of this method is shown in Figure 4.14.

Backup strategies

CUSTOMER ORDER DATA					
Monday		**Tuesday**		**Wednesday**	
Disk 1	Grandfather	Disk 2	Grandfather	Disk 3	Grandfather
Disk 2	Father	Disk 3	Father	Disk 1	Father
Disk 3	Son	Disk 1	Son	Disk 2	Son

Figure 4.14

Grandfather, father, son backup method

Network hardware and software componentss

Networks bring together a range of hardware and technologies, the following section will provide an overview of these.

Network cards

A network card – sometimes referred to as a Network Interface Card (NIC), plays a very important role in terms of connecting the cable modem and computer together. It will create a network interface through either wires or wireless technologies. The network card allows data to be transferred from your computer to another computer or device.

Workstations

A workstation can refer to a stand-alone computer or in terms of a network, a dumb terminal that is connected to it. In terms of networking, a network card will be necessary if a workstation is stand-alone in conjunction with communications software. In the case of a dumb terminal, a network card is integrated in the file server along with the communication software.

Servers

A server is a computer or a device that manages a range of network resources on a network. Examples of these can include:

- Print server – manages one or more printers
- File server – manages the storage of files
- Database server – processes and manages database queries
- FTP server – makes it possible to move one or more files securely between computers. It provides file security and organisation as well as transfer control.

Routers

Routers determine where to send the information from one computer to another. They are specialised computers that send the messages quickly to their destination/s along thousands of pathways.

A router serves two purposes, first it ensures that information doesn't go astray – this is crucial for keeping large volumes of data from clogging up connections and second, it ensures that the information does indeed make it to the intended destination.

In performing these two roles a router is invaluable. It joins networks together passing information from one to another, and also protects the networks from each other. It prevents the traffic from one, unnecessarily spilling over to another.

Regardless of how many networks are attached, the basic operation and function of the router remains the same. Since the Internet is one huge network made up of tens of thousands of smaller networks the use of routers is an absolute necessity.

In order to handle all the users of even a large private network, millions and millions of traffic packets must be sent at the same time. Some of the largest routers are made by Cisco Systems Inc.

Cisco's 'Gigabit Switch Router 12000 series' is a typical router system that is used on the backbone of the Internet. These routers use the same sort of design as some of the most powerful supercomputers in the world, a design that links many different processors together with a series of extremely fast switches.

The 12000 series uses 200-MHz MIPS R5000 processors, the same type of processor used in the workstations that generate much of the computer animation and special effects used in movies. The largest model in the 12000 series, the 12016, uses a series of switches that can handle up to 320 billion bits of information per second and, when fully loaded with boards, move as many as 60 million packets of data every second.

Hubs and switches

A hub is a connection point for devices in a network.

Hubs exist as layer one devices in the OSI model. Hubs cannot support very sophisticated networking in the physical layer and they do not read any of the data passing through them. Hubs are also not aware of the data's source or destination. A hub simply receives incoming packets, sometimes amplifies the electrical signal, and broadcasts these packets out to all devices on the network.

There are three main categories of hubs:

- active
- passive
- intelligent

Active hubs do amplify the electrical signal of incoming packets before broadcasting them out over the network. However, passive hubs do not perform this service. Intelligent hubs are 'stackable' in that they can place multiple units on top of each other to save space. Intelligent hubs can also include remote management services via SNMP and VLAN (virtual LAN) support.

Hubs remain a very popular device for small networks because of their low cost.

A switch is a device that filters and forwards pieces of a message referred to as a 'packet' within sections of a local area network.

There are a range of other hardware and software components and devices associated with networks. Examples of these can include connectors and cabling, Internet browsers, network operating systems, email and FTP software and firewalls.

Network operating systems

Network operating systems (NOS) like normal operating systems are essential for network start-up and operation. The type of NOS selected will vary depending upon the user or size of an organisation – scalability. For example, a small organisation running a peer-to-peer network might use Windows networking such as XP or NT. A large organisation, however, may have more complex networking requirements that would warrant the use of a more scalable NOS such as UNIX or Netware with dedicated network servers. Alternatively, they may be operating a combination of different network operating systems.

Broadband technologies are an essential part of networking, examples of these include ASDL and ISDN.

Activity 3

Discuss the different technologies of ISDN and ADSL.

Students should conduct research and produce a table to compare both of these technologies. The table should look at criteria such as:

* price
* asymmetry
* technology
* user types – home, business, etc.
* speed
* connection – permanent etc.

Setting up and using a local area network

There are a number of steps involved in setting up a local area network, in conjunction there are a number of practical activities that can be carried out to prepare you for this task.

Throughout this chapter, information has been provided on the basics of computer networks, types and topologies, features and services, hardware and software. All of this information can be used to provide the knowledge and skills needed to practically assemble and possibly install network components and devices.

The following sections will provide you with opportunities to attempt practical activities that will hopefully prepare you for your unit assessments.

Activity 4

Students should be introduced to a range of different network cables to include:

- thick Ethernet
- thin Ethernet
- shielded twisted pair (STP)
- unshielded twisted pair (UTP)
- fibre optic cables

Based on these different cable types, students should produce a table identifying what each cable is used for and the properties/characteristics of each cable type.

Practical activity – tutor led

Discuss and demonstrate how various cables can be assembled.

(1) Explain that this session has been set up to give students a more practical insight into network cabling
(2) Discuss any protocols involved with cable making and ensure that students are aware that health and safety procedures must be adhered to during the practical
(3) Some students will be in a position where they may not have assembled a cable before. Engage students in this process by setting up the resources to demonstrate how this can be achieved
(4) Set up an environment and demonstrate how to put a cable together – you may have to bring small groups of students up at a time to ensure that they can see clearly what steps are being followed
(5) Provide students with an opportunity to make their own cables and test them. Ensure that students take notes of the stages/steps involved
(6) The session should end with a review and consolidation followed by any questions about the activities undertaken.

Students are expected to set up, use and test a local area network. Through a series of practical and observation sessions, students could be shown how to carry out these activities.

(1) Demonstrate that you are aware of the necessary health and safety procedures that effect the set-up, use and testing of a local area network
(2) Demonstrate how a local area network can be set up in terms of adhering to health and safety, setting up and configuring hardware and software and knowing how to address any problems when and if they occur
(3) Demonstrate that you can use a range of network features to include: transferring files, allocating user rights, permissions and file space
(4) Produce test plans or appropriate testing documentation that demonstrates that testing has taken place. Testing should address both the functionality and the user interface.

Chapter 5

Database software

Database software is quite a common piece of applications software as it is used for a wide range of purposes in industry for data storage, manipulation and analysis purposes.

This short chapter will provide students with an overview of databases in terms of how they evolved, the principles of database design and offer support in terms of students creating their own databases.

The practical elements of database design will be discussed using a variety of screen shots and annotated graphics. In conjunction, a series of activities and tasks will be used to test the level of knowledge and understanding in this area.

When you complete this chapter you should be able to:

(1)   Understand the structure and principles of databases
(2)   Be able to create a simple database to meet user needs
(3)   Be able to create database queries
(4)   Be able to document a database.

Structure and principles of databases

Many definitions exist in terms of describing a database, some of which include: 'an electronic version of a filing cabinet', 'a computerised record-keeping system' and 'a shared collection of logically related data and a description of the data, designed to meet the information needs of an individual or organisation'.

Primarily a database is a combined storage and manipulation tool that forms the backbone to many organisational IT systems. Databases are used because they can:

- Process data fast and efficiently
- Process large volumes of data
- Reduce data redundancy due to its centralised approach
- Reduce repetitiveness of tasks for end-users
- Create a secure data environment.

Because of these qualities databases can be seen operating in a number of environments such as:

- Carrying out credit checks – see case study
- Surfing the Internet
- Checking flight availability at a travel agents
- Stock control at a supermarket
- Confirming patient details at a surgery.

It is hard to imagine what life was like without databases, however, data storage has always been achievable through alternative, manual methods and although not as efficient, their contribution to electronic storage is invaluable.

Storage systems

Data storage has always been possible through the use of manual systems consisting of in-trays, filing cabinets, index cards, etc., extending to file-based systems through to electronic storage systems such as databases and database management systems.

Manual storage data storage includes card index systems, in-trays and filing cabinets. Easy to access but with limited storage and no capabilities of cross-referencing.

Computerised version of the manual system
De-centralised approach – individual systems managing their own data

Sales   →   Customer information regarding orders and order history

→   Payment and transaction information regarding debtor and creditor listings

Accounts

Fully electronic centralised storage system
Database approach where all data is centrally deposited thus allowing easy access.

Figure 5.1

Development of data storage

Each generation of storage, manual through to electronic have contributed in some way to creating a more improved and faster way of storing and manipulating data.

The benefits of a manual system include its simplicity and hard copy formats, the limitations however include:

- inability to handle and process large volumes of data
- inadequate cross-referencing
- physical storage capacities
- security.

These limitations generating the need for a more efficient system. However, the underlying principles of manual storage – having individual data files stored in specific filing cabinets worked quite well in some areas, so therefore the next generation of storage was modelled on this, file-based systems being an early attempt to computerise the manual system.

File-based systems

The file-based system uses application programs to define and manage data, and it is modelled around the concept of decentralisation. Within an organisation each functional department generates their own data sets, this data would then be electronically stored, manipulated and accessed by personnel within that functional area. Figure 5.2 illustrates a typical file-based system.

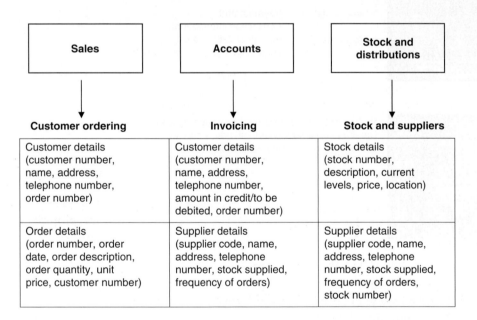

Figure 5.2

File-based system

This decentralised approach to data storage can create a number of problems that include:

* repetition of data within individual systems and across different systems
* segregation of data in different systems
* possible incompatibility issues

- data dependencies
- static application framework.

Data repetition can be seen within Figure 5.3.

Order details					
Order no.	Date	Description	Quantity	Unit price	Customer no.
P123/4O	23/06/03	2cm rubber rings	150	£0.24	JA/19009
R239/7G	24/06/03	2m^2 wire mesh sheets	30	£1.12	GH/34899
P349/9I	24/06/03	10cm plastic screw caps	100	£0.46	JA/19009
S754/8K	25/06/03	1m copper pipes	40	£1.07	DR/47886
HY492/0P	25/06/03	1m^2 insulating foam sheets	25	£0.89	DR/47886

Figure 5.3

Data repetition in file-based systems

Following on from file-based systems are database and database management systems.

Databases are made up of a number of different components that allow you to:

- Create tables, forms and reports
- Enter data into fields
- Select and edit records
- Manipulate data using a range of tools and techniques such as macros, filters, sort and queries, etc.
- Nominate a primary key
- Import graphics and data from other applications.

Some of these features will be explored further in this chapter.

Test your knowledge

(1) Identify four benefits of using a database approach
(2) Provide three examples of how a database can be used
(3) What is meant by a file-based system and identify two problems in using this approach?
(4) Why is data repetition a problem?
(5) What can a database allow you to do?
(6) Identify four features of a database system.

Creating a simple database

Creating a database is quite a straightforward task with the use of applications software such as Microsoft Access.

There are a number of stages that need to be addressed to create a database, these involve:

- the initial selection of a blank database screen
- creating a name for the database
- identifying the type(s) of input screen to be used
- identifying, selecting and modifying elements of the database.

The initial selection of a blank database screen, involves loading up the software and selecting a new database from the menu options as shown in Figure 5.4.

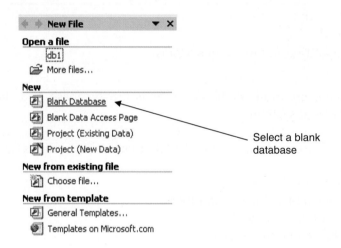

Figure 5.4

Selecting a blank database

Once a blank database has been selected, you will be required to give your database a name before proceeding to the main design screen.

For the purpose of demonstrating certain functions and features of databases, a sample database 'The Curious Book Shop' will be used throughout this chapter.

The Curious Book Shop will provide you with an opportunity to see how data can be stored within tables and forms, how information can be accessed, filtered and output to reports.

Figure 5.5 illustrates what happens once you have initially provided a name and saved your database. The screen identified is the main selection area for the design of the database.

Database – The Curious Book Shop

Figure 5.5
Main database selection area

Input forms

There are two types of input forms that can be used to type data directly into a database, these are:

- Tables
- Forms

Tables are set out in a grid/tabular format and provide an overview of the information for your database (single table at a time). The significance of tables is that you can create as many or as few as you require, each table having its own unique data set.

Using the example of The Curious Book Shop, tables can be established for the following areas as shown in Figure 5.6.

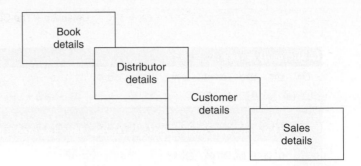

Figure 5.6

Sample tables for
The Curious Book Shop

Each of the tables can contain details about the information category; therefore the 'book table' might contain information such as:

<u>ISBN number</u> key field
Title
Author
Date of publication
Edition
Publisher
Category

To create a table you can either type information directly into a tabular template, or set up the design of the table by selecting field names and data types as shown in Figures 5.7 and 5.8.

```
▦ Table1 : Table
      Field1        Field2        Field3        Field4
▶  ⬆↓  Sort Ascending
   ⬇↓  Sort Descending
   ▤   Copy
   ▤   Paste
   ↔   Column Width...
       Hide Columns
   ▥   Freeze Columns
       Unfreeze All Columns
   ▥   Find...
   ▥   Insert Column
       Lookup Column...
   ▥   Delete Column
       Rename Column                          Columns can be renamed
                                              to represent the categories
                                              in the table
```

Figure 5.7

Table template

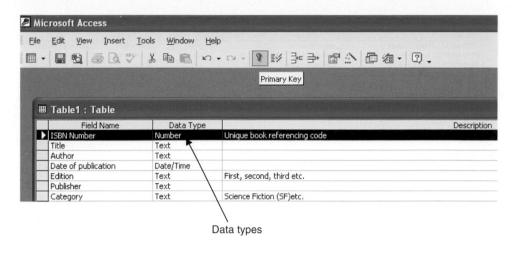

Data types

Figure 5.8

Table design template

What does this mean?

Data types: when you enter field names into the table design template, you are required to select an appropriate data type. For example, text, numeric, date/time.

Once the structure of the table has been set up, data can then be input as shown in Figures 5.9 and 5.10.

	Field Name	Data Type	Description
▼	ISBN Number	Text	Unique book referencing code
	Title	Text	
	Author(s)	Text	
	Date of publication	Text	
	Edition	Text	First, second, third etc.
	Publisher	Text	
	Category	Text	Science fiction (SF)

All data types have been changed to text in this example, the result of this shown in the table in 1.8.

Figure 5.9

Design view

Book details : Table							
ISBN Number	Title	Author(s)	Date of publication	Edition	Publisher	Category
1-1100-45569	Beyond space	Arthur Moon	2005	2nd	Black Hole	Science Fiction
1-2300-45667	Happy Holidays	Julia Lodge	2004	1st	Greenfields	Fiction
1-5678-00011	Coming Home	Margaret Housey	2006	1st	Picket Fence	Fiction
1-3423-39940	The Ultimate Guide to Shoes	Jonathon Heel	2005	2nd	Heel and Toe	Non-Fiction
1-2738-92738	History Through The Ages	Paul Battle	2005	1st	Round Table	History
1-4362-37829	A Secret Admirer	Jenny Love	2006	1st	Kissinger	Romance

Figure 5.10

Table with data

Identifying, selecting and modifying databases

Databases can be set up specifically to meet an end user's need. At the initial data input stage, data can be entered using a specific data type as previously explored, in addition field properties such as the length of a field can be changed, the default value, the fieldname can be re-named in conjunction with other modifications and validation rules can be set up as shown in Figure 5.11.

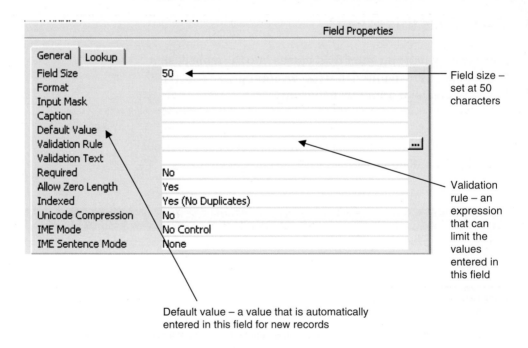

Figure 5.11

Field modifications

Checks

There are a number of checks that can be carried out to ensure that data has been input correctly. Some of these checks include the use of general tools such as spell check, other more specific checks can identify whether or not data has been set up correctly, that it is in the right format and that it carries out the required task/function requested. Table 5.1 provides an overview of some of the more specific checks that can be carried out.

Table 5.1

Data checks

Check	Purpose
Presence check	To ensure that certain fields of information have been entered, e.g. hospital number for a patient that is being admitted for surgery
Field/format/picture check	To ensure that the information that has been input is in the correct format and combination (if applicable), e.g. the surgery procedure has an assigned code made up of two letters and six numeric digits DH245639
Range check	To ensure that any values entered fall within the boundaries of a certain range, e.g. the surgery code is only valid for a 4-week period (1–4) therefore any number entered over 4 in this field would be rejected
Look-up check	To ensure that data entered is of an acceptable value, e.g. types of surgery can only be accepted from the list orthopaedic, ENT (ears, nose and throat) or minor
Cross-field check	To ensure that information stored in two fields matches up, e.g. if the surgeons initials are DH on the surgery code, they cannot represent the surgeon Michael Timbers but only Donald Hill
Check digit check	To ensure that any code number entered is valid by adding in an additional digit that has some relationship with the original code
Batch header check	To ensure that records in a batch, e.g. number of surgeries carried out over a set of period match the number stored in the batch header

Activity 1

(a) Design a database to meet one of the following user needs:
- A DVD/games rental shop
- A leisure club
- A holiday booking system

(b) The database should include at least three tables

(c) Each table should have at least 10 records in each

(d) Use both the table design and direct table entry methods.

Forms, reports and queries

Forms

Forms can be used to provide a more user-friendly method of inputting data. Forms can also be customised to include a range of graphics and background images. To create a form, you can select this option from the main menu as shown in Figure 5.12.

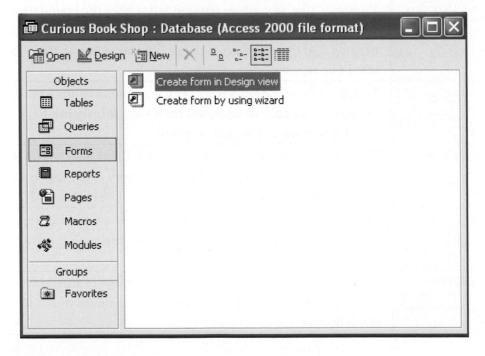

Figure 5.12

Selecting a form design

There are two options to form design, the first is to go onto the design palette and using the toolbox, set up each field, name it accordingly and position it as shown in Figure 5.12. The second way is to use the wizard function that allows you in a number of easy steps to select the fields and to choose a layout, style and label as shown in Figures 5.13–5.18.

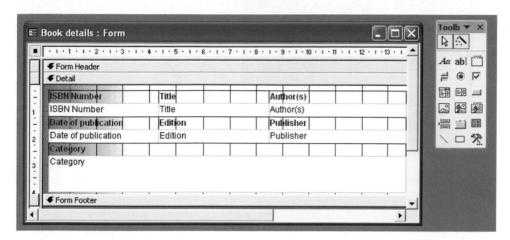

Figure 5.13
Form design view

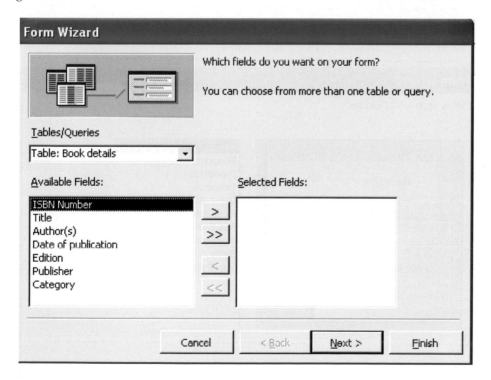

Figure 5.14
Form wizard step one – selecting fields

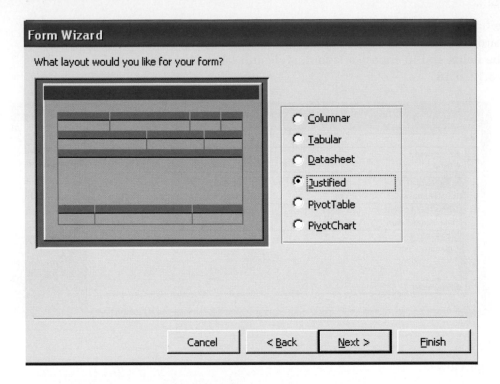

Figure 5.15

Form wizard step two – selecting the layout

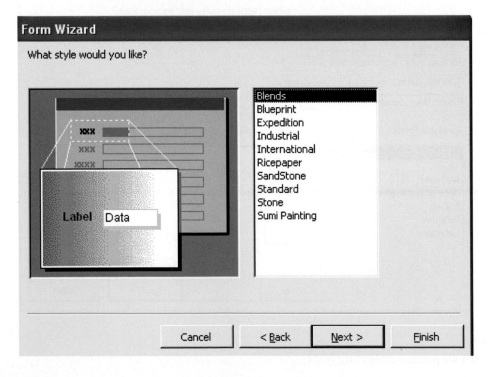

Figure 5.16

Form wizard step three – selecting the style

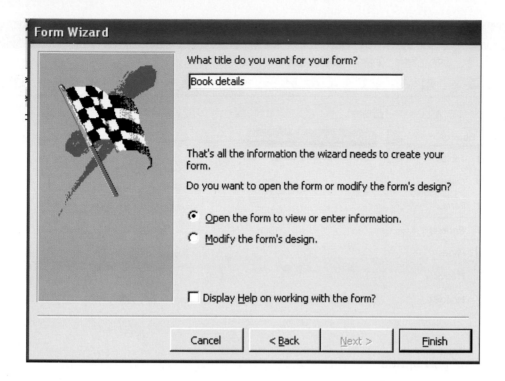

Figure 5.17

Form wizard step four – creating a name/label

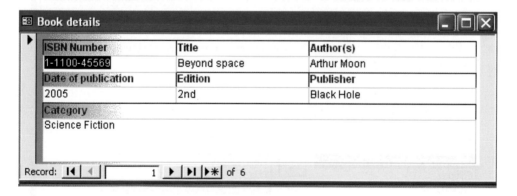

Figure 5.18

Complete form using wizard

Reports

Reports provide you with a consolidated set of information based on specific criteria that has been selected by the user. Reports can again be accessed from the main menu as shown in Figure 5.19.

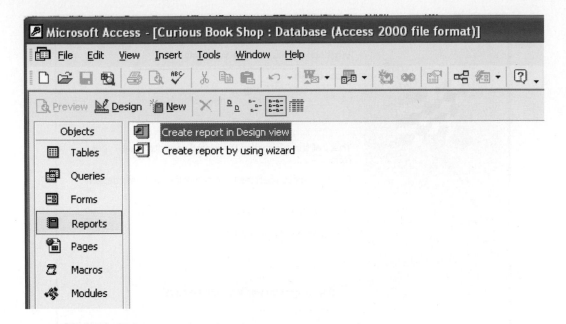

Figure 5.19

Selecting the report option

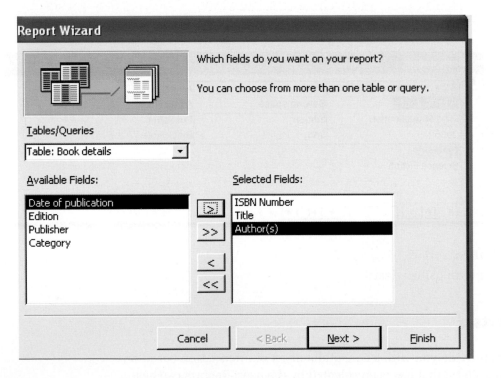

Figure 5.20

Creating a simple report using the wizard function

Book details

ISBN Number	1-2300-45667
Title	Happy Holidays
Author(s)	Julia Lodge
ISBN Number	1-1100-45569
Title	Beyond space
Author(s)	Arthur Moon
ISBN Number	1-5678-00011
Title	Coming Home
Author(s)	Margaret Housey
ISBN Number	1-3423-39940
Title	The Ultimate Guide to Shoes
Author(s)	Jonathon Heel
ISBN Number	1-2738-92738
Title	History Through The Ages
Author(s)	Paul Battle

Figure 5.21

Report based on the first four records

Queries

There are a range of queries that can be used on datasets to select specific data. Queries can be accessed from the query menu as shown in Figure 5.22.

Query and filter facilities

Microsoft Access has a number of query capabilities that fall into the category of Query-By-Example (QBE). QBE is used by entering example values directly into a query template and identifying the results in terms of the answer to a query. QBE can be used to ask questions about information held in one or more tables and to specify the fields that you want to appear in the answer. QBE can also be used to perform operations such as inserting and deleting records in tables, modifying the values of fields and creating new fields and tables.

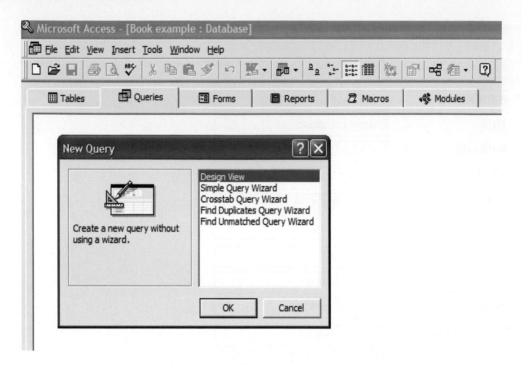

Figure 5.22
Query menu

Within Microsoft Access, there are a number of queries that can be performed. These include:

Select query

The most common type of query is the 'select query'. The function of the query is to retrieve data from one or more tables and display the results in a datasheet.

Totals query

It is useful to interrogate data and ask questions about groups of data such as 'how many students are enrolled on a particular course?' 'What is the average grade per cohort?' 'How many students went on to do another course following completion?' Totals queries can be used to perform calculations on groups of records. The types of calculation that can be performed include: Sum, Avg, Min, Max and Count.

Crosstab query

The crosstab query can be used to summarise data in a compact spreadsheet format. A crosstab query and its reporting facility produces a dynaset where the contents of one field are used as row headings. The cells of the query are then calculated on the basis of the fields matching the row and column fields. An example of a crosstab query can be seen in Figure 5.23.

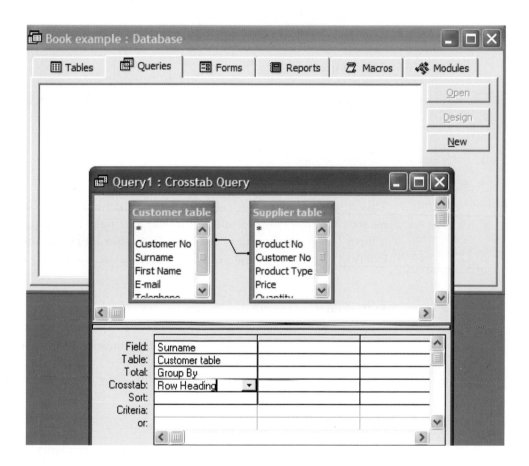

Figure 5.23
Crosstab query example

Parameter query

A parameter query displays one or more predefined dialogue boxes that prompt the user for a parameter value(s). Parameter queries are created by entering a prompt (enclosed in square brackets) in the 'criteria' cell for each field that is to be used as a parameter.

Find duplication query

This query determines whether or not duplicate records exist within a table, or whether or not records in a table share the same value.

Find unmatched query

This query finds records in one table that do not have related records in another table.

Action query

This query includes delete, append, update and make-table queries. The query can make changes in just one operation.

Autolookup query

This query will automatically fill in certain field values for a new record. When a value is entered in the join field in the query or in a form based on the query, Microsoft Access looks up and fills in existing information related to that value.

SQL query

This query is used to modify all the other queries identified and to set the properties of forms and reports.

Query example

Using the example of the Curious Little Book Shop, a query could be set up that would list the ISBN, Title and Author of each book, sorted alphabetically (ascending) by the title. The mechanics of this can be seen in Figure 5.24 and the actual evidence of running the query in Figure 5.25.

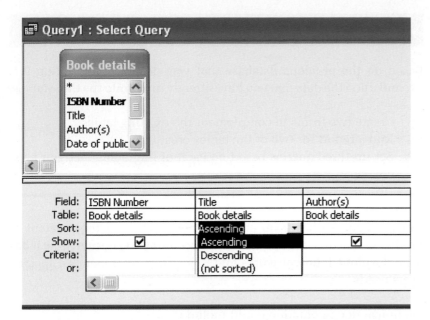

Figure 5.24

Designing a query

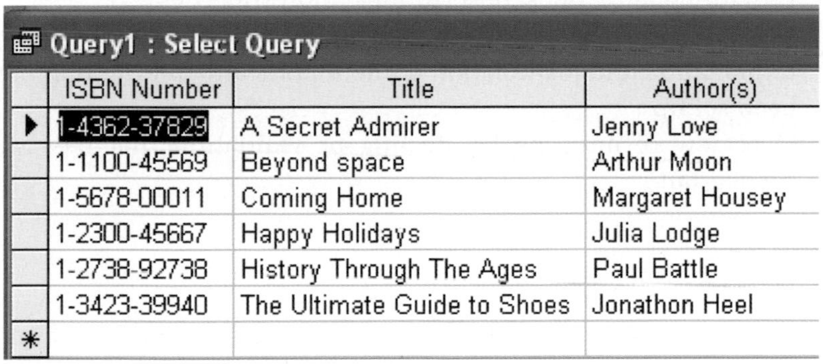

Figure 5.25

Completed query 'sorted alphabetically by book title'

Test your knowledge

(1) What is the purpose of a form and how does it differ from entering data into a table?
(2) Why might you want to use a report – provide four examples of report usage within databases?
(3) Provide two examples of when you could use a query?
(4) Provide a definition of the following query types:

- Action query
- Crosstab query
- Parameter query

Activity 2

Based on the previous database that was designed in Section 9.1, expand upon the data that you have already input into the three tables.

(a) Create two forms to complement the existing tables
(b) Run a report for two of the tables created
(c) Set up three queries based on each of the tables that you have created.

Documenting a database

Once a database has been created, there may be a requirement to produce some documentation to support the actual design, how it has been developed, how it works and to justify how it means a specific users needs.

Technical documentation could include:

- Providing fieldnames, descriptions and properties
- Description of the input forms and tables
- Explanation and justification of the reports and queries that have been set up
- Overview of any checks, testing or validation that has been carried out.

Chapter 6

Spreadsheet software

Spreadsheets can be used for a range of modelling purposes to support users in a range of environment to include finance, sales, production and general administration roles.

This short chapter will support you in the design and development of spreadsheets. You will be able to create spreadsheets that use a range of formulae, functions and features and through doing so, be able to interpret and analyse given data sets. In terms of presentation, this chapter will also demonstrate how spreadsheet data can be presented visually through the use of charts and graphs.

When you complete this unit you should be able to:

(1) Understand what spreadsheets are and how they can be used
(2) Create complex spreadsheets that use a range of formulae, functions and features
(3) Use spreadsheets to present, analyse and interpret data
(4) Check and document a spreadsheet solution.

Understanding spreadsheets

Spreadsheets provide a clear and consistent worksheet format that helps you understand and interpret the data. Spreadsheets are made up of 'cells', 'rows' and 'columns' as shown in Figure 6.1. Data can be typed in and stored as a skeleton template, further additions and updates can then be added. Once formulas have been set up on a spreadsheet, new data can be incorporated and updated easily, providing the user with current facts and figures.

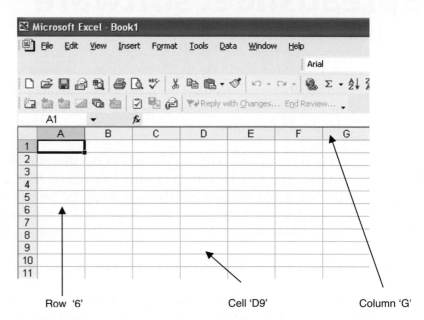

Figure 6.1

Spreadsheet template

Row '6'   Cell 'D9'   Column 'G'

Spreadsheets can be used as a modelling tool to provide users with a range of features to enable them to:

- Produce and display numerical, graphical and statistical data such as:
    - Sales forecasts
    - Profit and loss
    - General expenditure
    - Wage and salary information
    - Distribution facts
- Forecast information
- Calculate information
- Analyse information
- Automate procedures.

Spreadsheets can be used to support a range of user needs, an example of this can be seen in Figure 6.2, where a spreadsheet has been set up to support a 'sales forecast' system. The spreadsheet is broken down into months from January to August, and for each month actual sales figures have been recorded for a range of parts (A–H). In August, the

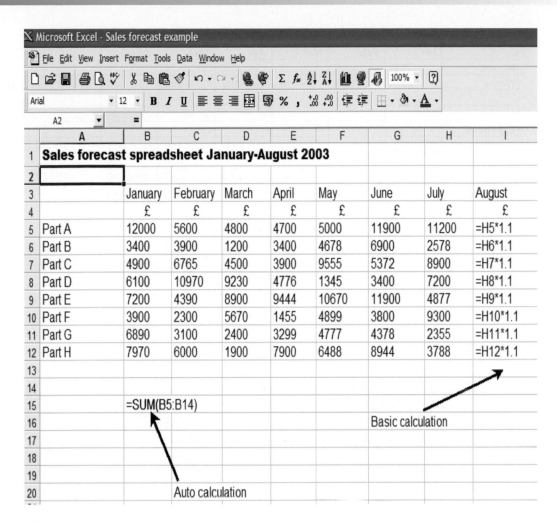

Figure 6.2

Sample spreadsheet to calculate and forecast information

spreadsheet figures have been presented in a calculation format to show a predicted rise from July's total sales.

Another use of a spreadsheet might be to show a monthly expenditure breakdown as shown in Figure 6.3.

	Jan	Feb	Mar	Apr	May	June	
Income	£	£	£	£	£	£	
Wages	620	620	620	620	620	620	
Expenses							
Entertainment	110	130	115	90	100	75	
Car tax	20	20	20	20	20	20	
Eating out	40	60	20	40	35	30	
Clothes	150	220	100	120	135	170	
Subtotal	320	430	255	270	290	295	
Balance	300	190	365	350	330	325	

Figure 6.3

Monthly expenditure breakdown

Test your knowledge

(1) What is meant by the following terms?
- A cell
- Workbook
- Column
- Row
(2) Identify four purposes for designing a spreadsheet
(3) What would the following action do =SUM(B4 + C4)?

Creating complex spreadsheets

There are a wide range of formulae and functions that can be used to enhance a spreadsheet. Simple mathematical formulae can include:

- Add (see Figure 6.4)
- Subtract (see Figure 6.5)
- Multiply (see Figure 6.6)
- Divide (see Figure 6.7)

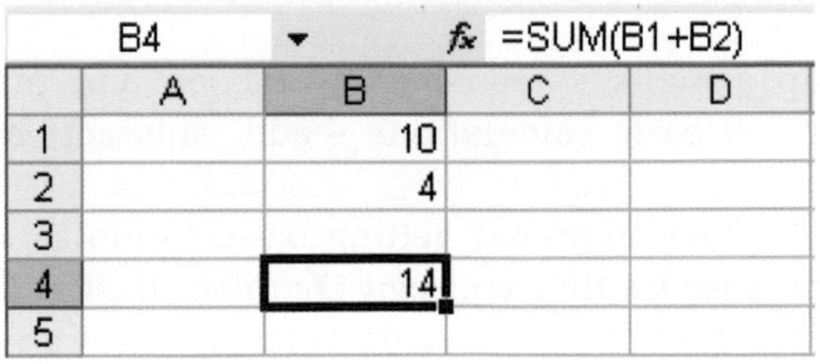

B4	▾	*fx* =SUM(B1+B2)	
	A	B	C	D
1		10		
2		4		
3				
4		14		
5				

Figure 6.4

Using the addition formulae

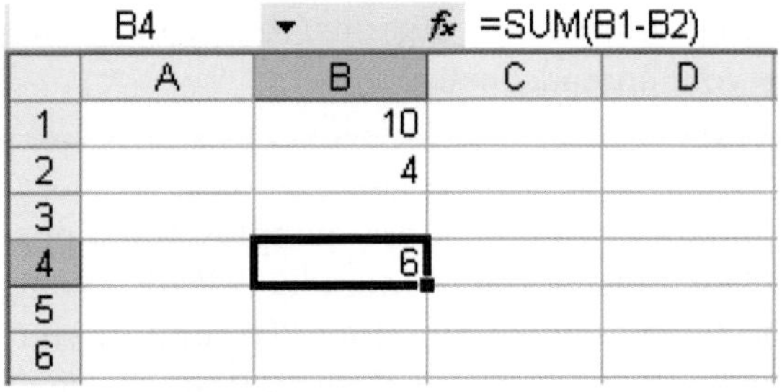

B4	▾	*fx* =SUM(B1-B2)	
	A	B	C	D
1		10		
2		4		
3				
4		6		
5				
6				

Figure 6.5

Using the subtraction formulae

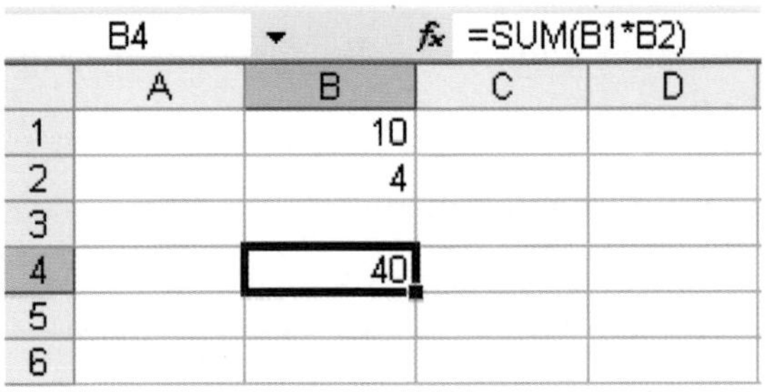

B4	▾	*fx* =SUM(B1*B2)	
	A	B	C	D
1		10		
2		4		
3				
4		40		
5				
6				

Figure 6.6

Using the multiply formulae

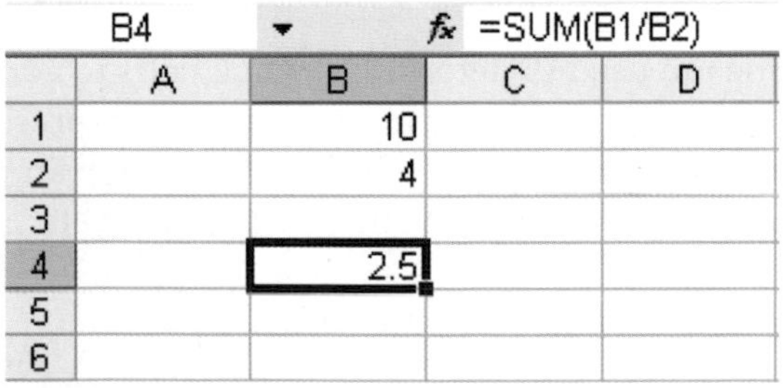

B4	▾	*fx* =SUM(B1/B2)	
	A	B	C	D
1		10		
2		4		
3				
4		2.5		
5				
6				

Figure 6.7

Using the divide formulae

Activity 1

(a) Open up a blank spreadsheet workbook and practice using some of the basic calculations – add, subtract, multiply and divide

(b) Once you have mastered getting basic formulas to work, set up a spreadsheet that you can complete over the next week. The spreadsheet should provide a breakdown of any money that you receive or spend during this period

(c) List each day of the week separately, and identify where your money has come from and what it is being spent on, e.g. bus fares, food, stationery, etc.

(d) Use a range of the calculations that you have practiced to enhance your spreadsheet.

There are a number of other more complex functions that can be used to model spreadsheets that include, SUMIF, average, min, max count, COUNTIF and logical functions. To support you in your own spreadsheet designs, an example of the SUMIF has been provided.

SUMIF

The SUMIF function adds the cells specified by a given criteria. The syntax used is:

SUMIF (range, criteria, sum range)

What does this mean?

Range is the range of cells that you want to apply the criteria against.

Criteria are used to determine which cells to add. Criteria – are the criteria in the form of a number, expression or text that defines which cells will be added. For example, criteria can be expressed as 40, "40", ">40", "widgets".

Sum ranges are the cells to sum.

Comments

- The cells in sum range are totalled, only if their corresponding cells in the range match the criteria
- If sum range is omitted, the cells in the range are totalled.

An example of the SUMIF function can be seen in Figure 6.8.

	A	B	C	D	E	F	G	H	I	J
1	Sales and commission for January 2003									
2										
3		January		Commission 1.5%						
4		£		£						
5	Part A	12,000		180						
6	Part B	3,400		51						
7	Part C	4,900		74						
8	Part D	6,100		92						
9	Part E	7,200		108						
10	Part F	3,900		59						
11	Part G	6,890		103						
12	Part H	7,970		120						
13										
14	Calculated commission for part sales that have exceeded £5,000 in January									£602.40

=SUMIF(B5:B12, "> 5000",D5:D12)

Figure 6.8

Example of the SUMIF function

A spreadsheet containing large volumes of data may not be easy to interpret. The graphical features offered by a spreadsheet, however, can be used to reflect certain data requirements. Some spreadsheet applications have built-in chart and graphic facilities to provide a more visual data interpretation, examples of these can be seen in Figure 6.9.

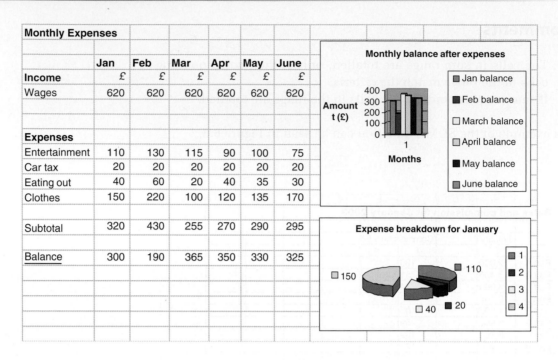

Figure 6.9

Examples of the charts and graphs offered by spreadsheets

Activity 2

(a) Using a spreadsheet, design a small system to meet one of the following user requirements:

   (i) Design a library system which can store information about DVDs and videos for a hire shop to include:
- Customer details
- DVD/Video details catalogue of titles
- Rental status

  (ii) Design a stock control system template which will automatically calculate stock levels and re-order levels, information should show:
- Period extending from January to June
- Stock items (fan belts, spark plugs, wheel nuts, fuses and tyres)
- Each stock items should have a stock level minimum requirement of 60 items
- When stock items reach below this level, an indicator should show the need to re-order

(b) Template designs should be clear and fully functional

(c) All data should be derived from you, and should be adequate enough to demonstrate the functionality of each system.

There are a range of other tools and techniques that can be applied to spreadsheet design and use. To improve the efficiency of a spreadsheet you can create shortcuts, to make your spreadsheet more automated. You could have auto-filled cells or link cells together between different workbooks. In terms of file management, you could ensure that all your spreadsheets have meaningful names and that you understand the folder structure if you want to edit, move or delete spreadsheet files.

Presenting data

Graphs and charts can provide a more visual overview of any data that has been entered in your spreadsheet. There are a number of graphs and charts that can be used, as shown in Figures 6.10–6.14.

Use spreadsheets to present, analyse and interpret data

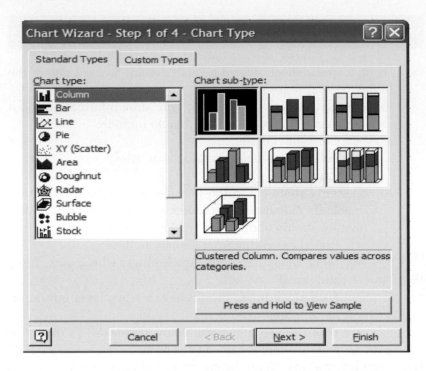

Figure 6.10
Chart types

Games consoles sales

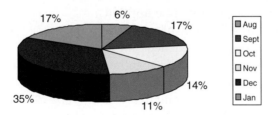

Each segment of the pie chart represents a percentage of games consoles sold for each month from August to January. The smallest segment is 6% for August and the largest is 35% for December.

Figure 6.11
Pie chart

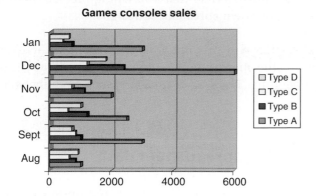

The bars on the graph each represent a type of games console ranging from A to D. The bar graph identifies for each month, how many of each console was sold.

Figure 6.12

Bar graph

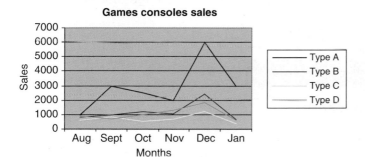

The line graph clearly plots the sales of each console from August to January. It is very evident that Type A console is the best seller and Type C console is the worst seller. From this graph it is also clear that in August, September and January sales were very similar for Types B, C and D.

Figure 6.13

Lino graph

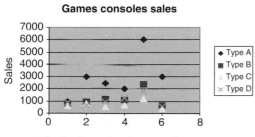

Scatter graphs are best used when there is a lot of numerical data that requires plotting to identify a correlation or pattern in the data. This specific scatter graph shows the pattern of sales for each month 1–6. In August it clearly shows that all four games console types had similar sales figures, however in December these are quite diverse.

Figure 6.14

Scatter graph

In order to support you in presenting data, a range of tools and techniques will be demonstrated so that you can appreciate how these can be applied to your own spreadsheet designs.

This practical section will provide you with examples and screenshots of some of the more popular tools and techniques used in spreadsheet modelling. The screenshots are taken from the software 'Microsoft Excel'.

Enter and editing spreadsheet data

To enter data into a spreadsheet, click on the appropriate cell which is referenced by a number and a letter, e.g. A1, B3, C2, etc. in the example shown in Figure 6.15. You can see that data entered in cell E5 '1888' appears in the formula bar at the top. If you wanted to change the data for cell E5, you would click on that cell and type in new data, or type the data directly into the formula bar.

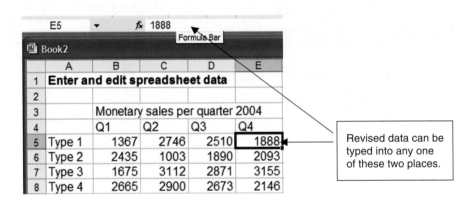

Figure 6.15

Entering and editing data

Formatting spreadsheets

The formatting menu (Figure 6.16) provides a range of options that can be selected to enhance your spreadsheet. The examples provided in this section will look at formatting of cells, the auto format and conditional formatting features. It is suggested that you experiment with the other format options when you do your own designs.

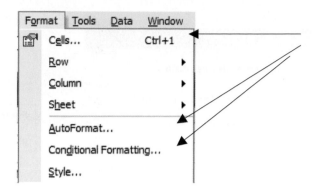

Figure 6.16

Format menu

You can identify whether you require individual cells, rows, columns or sheets to be formatted.

Using the 'cells' option and the 'number' function within it, it is easy to select data values and set them to two decimal places as shown in three easy steps as shown in Figures 6.17–6.19.

Step one

	A	B	C	D	E
1	**Enter and edit spreadsheet data**				
2					
3		Monetary sales per quarter 2004			
4		Q1	Q2	Q3	Q4
5	Type 1	1367	2746	2510	1888
6	Type 2	2435	1003	1890	2093
7	Type 3	1675	3112	2871	3155
8	Type 4	2665	2900	2673	2146

Enter the data to be formatted

Figure 6.17

Data to be formatted

Step two

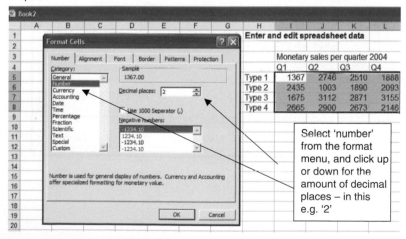

Select 'number' from the format menu, and click up or down for the amount of decimal places – in this e.g. '2'

Figure 6.18

Selecting the decimal function from the format menu

Step three

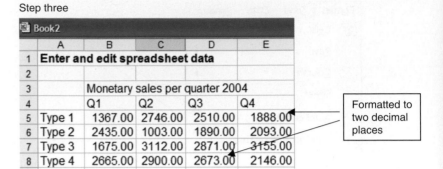

Figure 6.19

Data formatted to two decimal places

Formatted to two decimal places

Other formatting functions by 'cell' include:

- Format by alignment (Figure 6.20)
- Font formatting (Figure 6.21)
- Border formatting (Figure 6.22)
- Creating patterns (Figure 6.23)
- Cell protection (Figure 6.24)

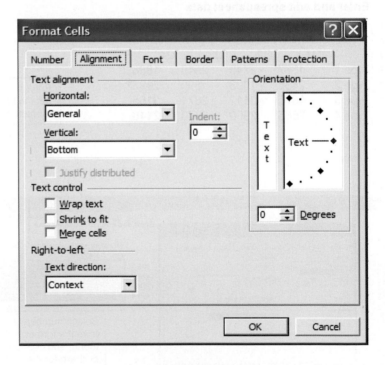

Figure 6.20

Alignment formatting

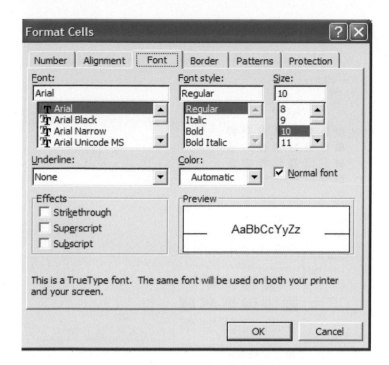

Figure 6.21

Font formatting

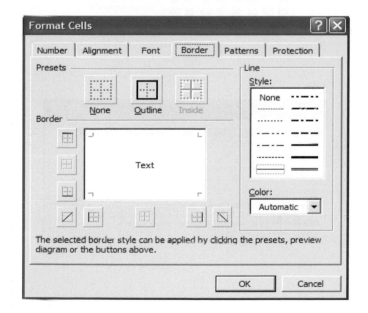

Figure 6.22

Border formatting

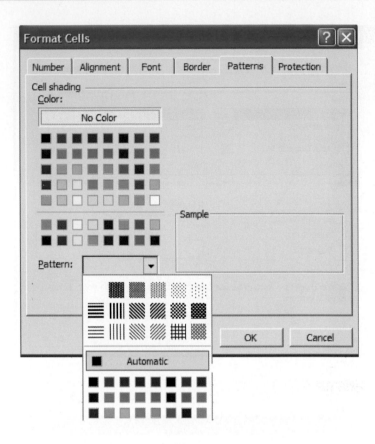

Figure 6.23
Using patterns

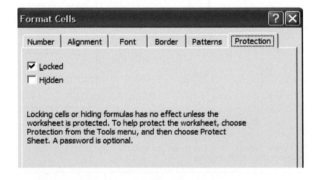

Figure 6.24

Applying protection to a
cell or formula

Auto formatting

The 'auto format' function will apply a customised template over your
own spreadsheet as shown in Figure 6.25.

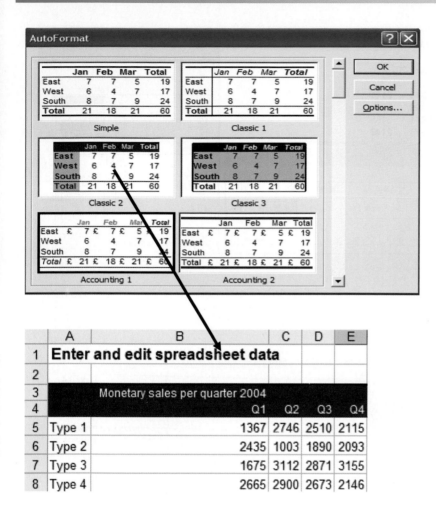

Figure 6.25
Auto formatting

Conditional formatting

This function allows you to select the type of formatting that wish to be applied to certain data, under certain conditions. In the example shown in Figure 6.26, all data between the value of 2000 and 3000 has been placed in bold.

Filters

Applying a filter will allow you to focus on a particular section of data – screening off the rest as shown in Figures 6.27 and 6.28.

By applying a filter to the 'total' column, it allows me to select which totals I want to view – in this case those for '8738' relating to 'type 1' items.

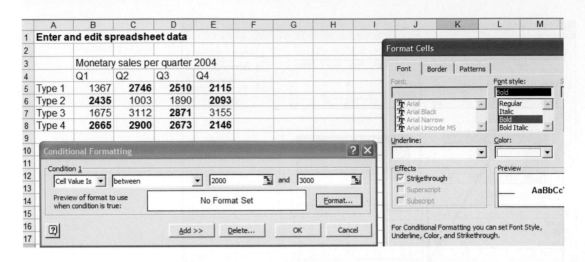

Figure 6.26

Example of conditional formatting

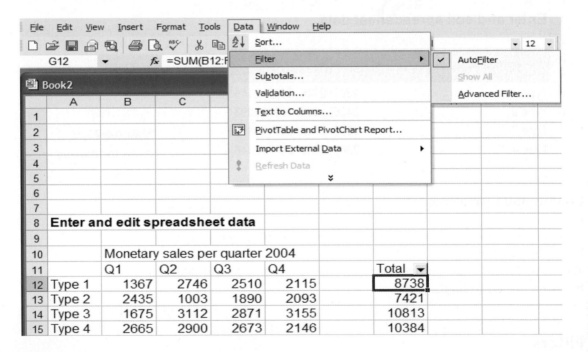

Figure 6.27

Selecting a filter

Sorting data

The 'sort' function will allow you to sort information in ascending or descending order. You can select which data you want to sort by

Enter and edit spreadsheet data						
	Monetary sales per quarter 2004					
	Q1	Q2	Q3	Q4		Total ▾
Type 1	1367	2746	2510	2115		

(All)
(Top 10…)
(Custom…)
7421
8738
10384
10813

Figure 6.28
Applying a filter

clicking on each criteria – 'sort by', 'then by', 'then by' as shown in Figure 6.29.

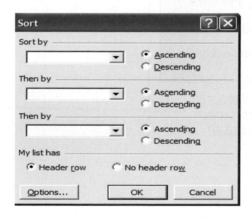

Figure 6.29
Sort function

Example – sorting student enrolment information alphabetically by surname (unsorted version in Figure 6.30, sorted versions in Figures 6.31 and 6.32).

Student enrolment information

Surname	First name	Enrolment number
James	Stewart	SJ/1267OP
Harrison	Charlotte	CH/5374LP
Michaels	John	JM/2900GL
Davids	Rebecca	RD/6729HN
Smyth	Pippa	PS/2773BN
Peterson	Jack	JP/7002LS
Morris	Joan	JM/3544NM
Jacobs	Mary	MJ/1003RT

Figure 6.30
Unsorted data set

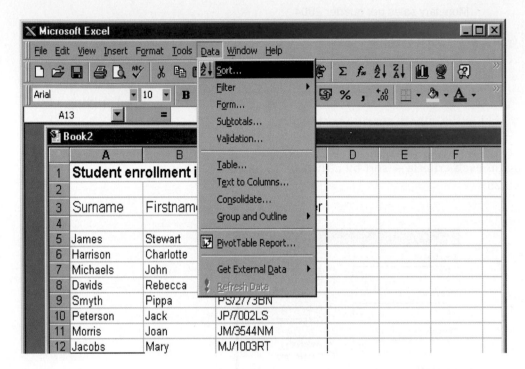

Figure 6.31

Using the sort function

Student enrolment information

Surname	First name	Enrolment number
Davids	Rebecca	RD/6729HN
Harrison	Charlotte	CH/5374LP
Jacobs	Mary	MJ/1003RT
James	Stewart	SJ/1267OP
Michaels	John	JM/2900GL
Morris	Joan	JM/3544NM
Peterson	Jack	JP/7002LS
Smyth	Pippa	PS/2773BN

Figure 6.32

Sorted data set

Activity 3

Scenario

You work in a large stationery shop. Your role is to help the supervisor with the stock take and the re-ordering of stationery supplies. Although you are just a trainee at present, it is expected that you will be promoted to the supervisor role within six months.

Part of the supervisor's responsibilities is to try and identify what supplies will be in demand over a four-week period. At certain times of the year it is quite easy to do this – for example between August and September the demand for 'back to school' stationery is very high, this is also the case in January when students return to school and college after the Christmas break.

In order to assist you in your decision-making process, about what stock items should be ordered, the manager of the shop has started to design a spreadsheet based on the budget of £250. The items and their associated costs are listed below:

Stationery items	Unit price (£)
Ring binder	0.79
A4 Pad	1.25
A5 Pad	1.05
Pack 10 clear wallets	2.15
Pack 5 cardboard folders	1.79
Pack 4 pens	0.99
Stationery set	3.75
Pack 3 ruled pads	2.00
Pack 3 storage boxes	3.45

Tasks

(1) Look at the sample spreadsheet that has been created and complete the model using various combinations of stationery item quantities

	B	C	D	E	
1			Stock budget		
2					C4*D4
3	**Item**	**Price**	**Number**	**Cost**	Formulas need to be added for the cost column
4	Ring binder	0.79	0.00	0.00	
5	A4 Pad	1.25	0.00	0.00	
6	A5 Pad	1.05	0.00	0.00	
7	Pack 10 clear	2.15	0.00	0.00	
8	wallets				
9	Pak of 5 folders	1.79	0.00	0.00	
10	Pack of 4 pens	0.99	0.00	0.00	
11	Stationary set	3.75	0.00	0.00	
12	Pack of 3 ruled	2.00	0.00	0.00	
13	pads				
14	Pack of 3	3.45	0.00	0.00	A total column
15	storage boxes				needs to be added
16					to check that the cost falls within
17	**Enter the number of unit stationary items**				the £250 budget
18	**required to make up the £250 budget**				

Figure 6.33

Sample spreadsheet

(2) The spreadsheet that has been set up by the manager is incomplete, formulas should be included to total up each stationery item and a total cost needs to be included to check that the items ordered falls within the £250 parameter

(3) Once the spreadsheet has been set up, project the information visually in a graph of your choice

(4) Identify other modelling techniques that can be used with this spreadsheet.

Once you have designed a model and analysed the results, you will need to consider whether or not the results meet the original specifications, for example:

A spreadsheet for a toy company is required that can provide the following information, easily.

Requirements

(i) The spreadsheet can display a breakdown of the sales for each toy over a six-month period (monetary and quantity based)

(ii) Average sales can be calculated for each month

(iii)   Trends in sales can be identified over the period
(iv)   If a new toy was introduced onto the market, you would be able to forecast a selling price for the next six-month period based on the average selling price for the month plus 10%.

When you have designed your own model(s), you need to ensure that they are working correctly and that they meet the original design requirements. You may find that although a solution has been provided, alternatives may also exist that may be more cost-effective, labour saving or resourceful. Therefore, you will need to incorporate a framework for scrutinising and analysing your model that shows that the decision-making process that you have undertaken identifies:

(1)   Which decisions produce the best results?
(2)   What alternatives you have looked at?
(3)   What differentiates the alternatives from the solution/s that you have chosen?
(4)   What, if anything does the model not take into account – what are its limitations?
(5)   What the impact of these limitations or constraints might have in the short- and long-term?

Checking and documenting a spreadsheet solution

Once a spreadsheet has been developed and tested, supporting documentation could be produced to emphasis the key features of the design and to identify how the design meets the original aims and objectives.

Documentation that might be used to support this spreadsheet could include a short report outlining the initial requirements, aims and objectives. Various graphs and charts could also be added to provide more of a visual overview. If the model is quite complex, it might also be appropriate to design a user guide.

Recommendations should also be included within any documentation that supports a spreadsheet model. These will aid the end user in understanding and appreciating the complexity of the model. Any recommendations should include:

* Summary of the current situation
* Sources and alternatives you have considered
* Other factors that you took into consideration
* The methods you used to reach your decision
* Your decision
* Justification of your decision, supported by evidence of the decision-making process.

Evaluating models

To evaluate whether a model has been successful, you would have to base the decision on whether or not the specified requirements have been met. If information is displayed accordingly and techniques have been applied to calculate average sales, different trends and a predicted sale of a new toy on the market, then yes, the model is a success.

When evaluating a model(s) you should consider:

- How well the model has performed?
- To what extent the model has helped you in making the right decision?
- What else you would like the model to do?
- Does the model need extending, and if so, how?

One tool that can be used to support you in preparing your evaluation is a checklist which can be drawn up that allows you to address each of these considerations, for example, using the 'toy company' brief:

Toy Company Model Evaluation		
		Met
Requirements	**Yes**	**No**
The spreadsheet can display a breakdown of the sales for each toy over a six-month period (monetary and quantity based).		
Average sales can be calculated for each month		
Trends in sales can be identified over the period		
If a new toy was introduced onto the market, you would be able to forecast a selling price for the next six-month period based on the average selling price for the month plus 10%		
The spreadsheet can display a breakdown of the sales for each toy over a six-month period (monetary and quantity based).		
Functionally and appearance: 1. Is the spreadsheet easy to use? 2. Is the spreadsheet clear and easy to read? 3. Are the colours and font styles acceptable? 4. Do the formulas all work? 5. Are more formulas needed? *Comments:*		

Figure 6.34

Model evaluation checklist

	Within 6 months	Within a year	Within 1–3 years
Does the model need extending?			
Comment on the way in which the model will need extending:			
Final comments:			

Figure 6.34

continued

Chapter 7

ICT graphics

Graphics are now an essential part of communication. They bring colour, a different level of understanding, clarity, structure and dynamics to a wide range of documents, displays, materials and presentations.

The use of graphics in ICT has become more popular due to the wide range of software applications available to produce, download and import images. In conjunction, the hardware devices required to support the production of a graphic such as digital cameras, colour printers, scanners and high capacity storage devices have fallen in price, which means that a range of users can now have access to these as opposed to professionals such as graphic designers, production teams, media personnel and engineers.

This chapter will provide an overview of graphics in terms of how they can be produced and the hardware and software needed to produce them. In addition, techniques to facilitate the design, file format and handling and graphic enhancements will also be explored.

When you complete this chapter you should be able to:

(1) Understand the hardware and software required to work with graphic images
(2) Create and modify graphic images to meet a user need
(3) Select, acquire and import appropriate images to enhance a document.

Hardware requirements

There are a wide range of hardware devices that are required to support the design transfer and storage of graphics. Some of these devices are quite standard and are usually integrated within a computer system, others are peripheral items that can be purchased to enhance any graphics produced and the output of any designs.

Hardware that is required to work with graphic images can be seen in Figure 7.1.

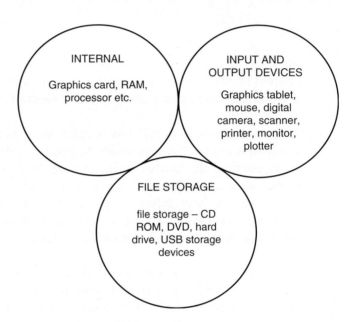

Figure 7.1

Hardware required for graphic images

The hardware required can be divided into three areas, internal hardware that usually comes as standard with most computers. However, the range of graphics cards, RAM and processing speed does vary amongst systems. The higher the capacity of the machine and the faster the system usually means more expense.

What does this mean?

RAM (Random Access Memory) is the main store. This is the place where programs and software once loaded is stored. When the CPU runs a program, it fetches the program instructions from RAM and executes them. RAM can have instructions read from it by the CPU and also it can have numbers or other computer data written to it by the CPU.

RAM is volatile which means that the main memory can be destroyed, either by being overwritten as new data is entered for processing or when the machine is switched off. Therefore, it is not practical to store data files and programs permanently in the main memory.

Input and output devices for the use and design of graphics can be quite standard such as monitors, printers and scanners, other devices, however, can be quite specialist such as digital cameras, graphics tablets and plotters.

Specialist graphics devices

Digital cameras

A digital camera stores images digitally as opposed to recording them on a film. Once a picture has been taken it can be stored and viewed instantly, downloaded onto a computer, modified using graphics software and then saved or printed. One of the main benefits of using a digital camera is the processing cost. Unlike a conventional camera the images/photographs do not have to be taken away and processed, they can simply be downloaded and printed on a range of paper or specialist photo paper for a minimal amount.

Figure 7.2
Digital camera

A graphics tablet, also referred to as digitiser, touch tablet or just tablet is an input device that enables a user to enter drawings and sketches into a computer. The tablet consists of an electronic tablet and a pen.

Plotters

Plotters work by moving a pen across the surface of a piece of paper. Plotters can produce quite complex line art images designed around vector-based graphics.

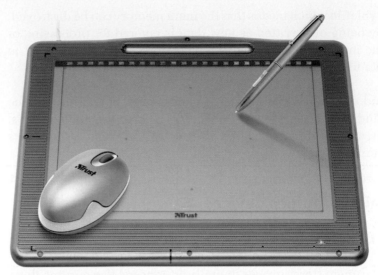

(a) Trust TB-4200 wireless scroll tablet

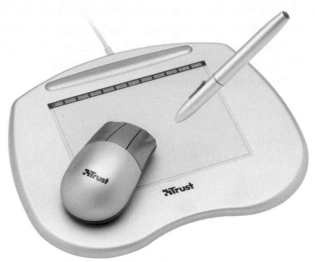

Figure 7.3

Graphics tablets
(Courtesy of Trust)

(b) Trust TB-2100 wireless tablet

File storage

There are a range of file storage devices available, some of these are integrated within the main system, and others are more portable such as UCB storage devices.

Activity 1

There is a range of file storage available to support graphics.

(a) Carry out research to enable you to complete the table
(b) Complete the table below to provide valid and accurate comparisons between the different types of file storage.

File storage type:	Storage capabilities:	Price range:	Benefits:	Limitations:
Floppy disk				
CD				
DVD				
USB Pen				

Software requirements

There is a wide range of software available to support the creation of graphics. This range of software can be divided into the following classifications:

- Vector graphics software – e.g. CorelDRAW, Visio, etc.
- Bitmap software – e.g. Paintshop Pro and Paint
- Manipulation software – e.g. Photoshop and Photoshop Elements
- Embedded software – e.g. image viewers, drawing tools, photo galleries, etc.

Vector graphics software

Vector graphics use geometrical figures and shapes such as points, lines, curves and polygons to create images in computer graphics. The images are made up of individual scalable objects, these objects being defined by equations as opposed to pixels.

The benefits of using vector graphics:

- Scalability – the size of the image can be increased or decreased to any degree without distortion in the lines
- Not restricted to rectangular shapes (unlike bitmap), they can be placed over objects, the objects beneath showing through
- Can easily be converted to bitmap format
- Cartoon like appearance – good for games design.

There is a range of vector-based software available that includes: CorelDRAW, Visio and Adobe Illustrator.

Bitmap software

Bitmap images are generated from pixels, these are tiny dots of individual colour that make up what you see on a screen. The tiny dots of colour come together to form an image. The typical computer monitor has 72 or 96 pixels per inch, depending on the monitor and screen settings.

Typical bitmap software includes: Paintshop Pro, Paint, etc.

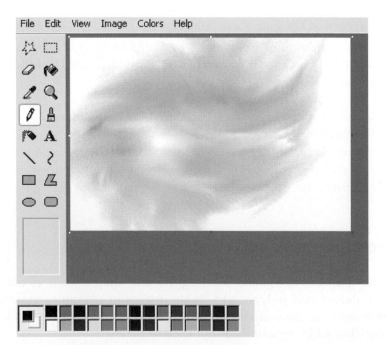

Figure 7.4
Paint screenshot

Manipulation software

Manipulation software includes packages such as Photoshop and Photoshop elements, where images that have been created can be manipulated in a number of ways in terms of adding special effects, changing the size – cropping, rotating, scaling, etc.

Embedded software

This type of graphics software is embedded within another application, such as drawing tools within a word processing package or tools such as image viewers, photo galleries, etc.

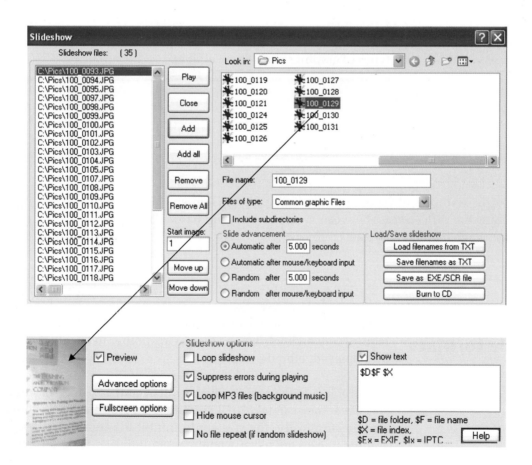

Figure 7.5

InfranView – Example of image software

Activity 2

This group activity is designed to get students looking at and reviewing a variety of graphics software and evaluating the qualities of each.

(a) Divide the class into four groups, each group should be given a software category:
- Vector
- Bitmap
- Manipulation
- Embedded

(b) The group should spend at least 45 min looking at the functions and features of a piece of software that fits within their category

(c) Using a flip chart sheet, the group should then design an information sheet based on their software category that can be presented to the rest of the class.

This activity should promote a better understanding of the different types of graphics software available.

Test your knowledge

(1) Provide examples of vector, bitmap, manipulation and embedded software
(2) What is the difference(s) between vector and bitmap-based software?
(3) What is meant by 'embedded' software?

File handling and file formats

Graphics can be saved in a number of formats and in some cases require conversion from one format to another to enable the image to be displayed, edited or stored.

The problem with graphics files is the overall size and the amount of space that they can take up. In addition if a graphics file is going to be sent electronically, the size could inhibit file transfer which is why graphic images are usually compressed into a suitable format.

There are a range of different file formats, some of which are software package specific, others are more generic as shown in Table 7.1.

As part of good file management procedures it is sensible to check that any data, information or graphics have been stored securely, in a place that can be easily identified and accessed. A checklist similar to the one provided in Table 7.2 could indeed support a user in doing this.

Table 7.1

Generic file formats

Format abbreviation	Format name	Format description
.bmp	Bitmap	Windows or OS/2 bitmap file. Mono with colour options of 4-bit, 8-bit and 24-bit
.gif	CompuServe Graphics Interchange Format	Uses a palette of up to 256 colours, popular with website graphics
JPEG	Joint Photographer's Exchange Graphic is a compressed raster image format file	Used for web-based distribution and display of photographic quality images
TIFF	Tagged Image File Format	Mainly used for exchanging documents between different applications and different computer platforms

Table 7.2

Criteria that can be followed for good file management procedures

Category	Criteria	Adhered to	
		Yes √	No ×
File management	Save work regularly		
	Use sensible filenames		
	Set up directory/folder structures to organise files		
	Make backups		
	Choose appropriate file formats		
	Limit access to confidential or sensitive files		
	Use effective virus protection		
	Use 'read me' files where appropriate to provide technical information e.g. system requirements		

Test your knowledge

(1)   Why do graphics files need to be compressed?
(2)   Name three types of file formats
(3)   Identify four elements of 'file management'
(4)   Why is it important to follow good file management procedures?

Creating and modifying graphics

Graphics and end-users

Graphics can take on a number of different formats to incorporate a range of drawings, pictures, graphs, charts, etc. as shown in Figure 7.6.

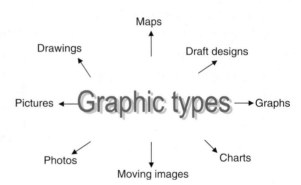

Figure 7.6
Types of graphics

The use of graphics is far-reaching and they can be found in almost every working environment, examples of which can be seen below:

*   Building – house builder will require graphics in terms of a house or site development plan
*   A car manufacturer – designs for a new vehicle model
*   Medicine – drawings may be required to support doctors such as pictures of the human anatomy, bone structure, muscle areas, etc.
*   Corporate organisations – organisation charts
*   Retail – sales forecast charts and graphs
*   Media – photographic images used for marketing purposes.

Graphics can command more of a positive and motivated response to an issue as opposed to information presented in a written format. Pictures, graphics, charts and moving images may offer more clarity and aid more understanding of an issue than lengthy written explanations. Too many visuals, however, may distract the audience from the core information.

Activity 3

To emphasise the importance of graphics, carry out the following exercise in groups of three.

(a) One person within the group should draw up a set of written instructions of how to get from one familiar location to another, A–B
(b) In collaboration with the second team member, the instructions should be read out, to enable them to draw a map of how to get from A to B
(c) Together both team members should then present the two formats of instructions to the third team member so that they can identify which of the two formats is more appropriate and clearer to understand, giving reasons.

Graphics are used for a number of different purposes that ranges from providing a general understanding such as a picture of the human anatomy adding humour such as cartoons and comic strips, providing clarity to a situation through the use of a picture, chart or diagram.

Maps

Maps are an excellent example of a graphic. There are a wide variety of maps available all of which provide visual guidance and direction to a specific geographic location or topic (mind map).

Figure 7.7
Map of Europe

Draft designs

Draft designs can include a range of sketched or early version drawings that are created to provide an idea about a concept. Examples could include:

- Car designs
- House designs
- Project designs
- Engineering designs for new engines etc.

Activity 4

The example of the draft design for a housing development visually indicates the plans of new houses to be built. Using a similar scale, design a development to accommodate the following requirements:

(i)   Twelve three bedroom, seven four bedroom and six five bedroom houses

(ii) All of the five bedroom houses should have a double garage, three of the four bedroom houses should have a single garage and four of the two bedroom houses should have a single garage

(iii) Swimming pool and two tennis courts

(iv) Courtyard environment

(v)   Good road links and pathways

(vi) Lots of trees and foliage.

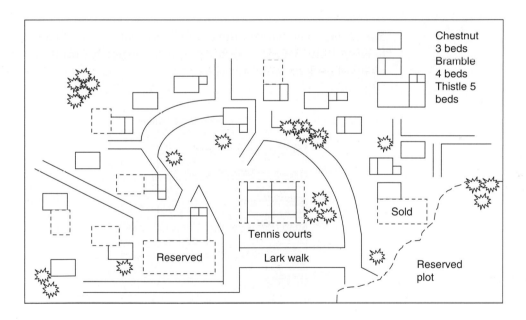

Figure 7.8

Draft design for a housing development – Forest Development Phase II

Graphs and charts

Graphs and charts are used to provide visual support to data and tables providing a clear breakdown of key data components.

Different graphs and charts are used to represent different information, some of the more popular ones in use include:

Pie chart Each segment of the pie chart represents a percentage of games consoles sold for each month from August to January. The smallest segment is 6% for August and the largest is 35% for December.

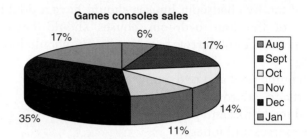

Figure 7.9

Pie chart

Bar graph The bars on the graph represent a type of games console ranging from A to D. The bar graph identifies for each month, how many of each console was sold.

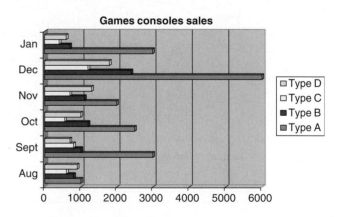

Figure 7.10

Bar graph

Line graph The line graph clearly plots the sales of each console from August to January. It is very evident that Type A console is the best seller and Type C console is the worst seller. From this graph, it is also clear that in August, September and January, sales were very similar for Types B, C and D.

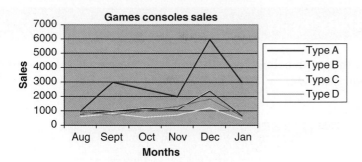

Figure 7.11

Line graph

Scatter graph Scatter graphs are best used when there is a lot of numerical data that requires plotting to identify a correlation or pattern in the data. This specific scatter graph is illustrating the pattern of sales for each month 1–6. In August, it clearly shows that all four games console types had similar sales figures, however in December, these are quite diverse.

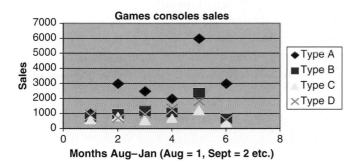

Figure 7.12

Scatter graph

Activity 5

Using the graph below, identify four key elements of information that are being shown.

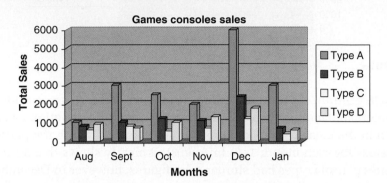

Figure 7.13

Activity graph

The graph can provide a great deal of information about sales of games consoles. However, graphics alone may not be sufficient. To provide a more detailed analysis of games console sales, raw data may also need to be included so that more specific information can be gathered, such as calculating average sales over a set period.

Activity 6

Sales of Games Consoles 2005/2006		Aug	Sept	Oct	Nov	Dec	Jan
Type A		1000	3000	2500	2000	6000	3000
Type B		800	1000	1200	1100	2400	700
Type C		600	800	550	700	1200	400
Type D		900	700	1000	1300	1800	600

Figure 7.14

Activity table

Using the table above present the information in two different graphical formats.

Moving images

Moving images, film and video footage are probably the most dynamic form of graphics. The incorporation of sound, colour and movement make moving images ideal for advertisements and marketing purposes.

Photos, drawings and pictures

These are all variations on the same theme, the main difference being that photographs are taken using some form of camera, phone, digital camera, etc., where as a drawing or picture implies a hand created image. Drawings and pictures can also include cartoons.

User requirements

The use of graphics can depend upon the type of message that needs to be conveyed. There may be a specific target audience that will then dictate the type of graphic to be used. For example, if you were trying to market a new toy to pre-school children, the graphics used might be big, bold and colourful possibly using a cartoon brand known to this age group, e.g. a well-known Disney character or a character from a children's programme. If however, you were trying to sell a product to a new company, charts and graphs might be more appropriate to identify current market share, predicted sales and forecasted profit over a certain period.

Graphics can therefore be constrained by the proposed target audience, the format may be being dictated by the occasion or formality. There are a number of other factors that can impose some form of constraint on the type of graphic(s) to be used, these can include:

* Cost – the design of certain types of graphics especially moving images can be beyond the intended budget for a user or organisation
* House style – organisations tend to have corporate logos and graphics that are used on a range of business documents and promotional materials
* Format – colour, size and type, the graphic once it has been created in a certain way may not be altered. Changing the colour or size may distort the graphic in some way making it unusable
* Hardware and software – the creation of a graphic is indeed constrained by the technology being used to create it. If a basic

graphics package is being used, then only a basic graphic may be produced. If there is inadequate storage or memory, any graphics created might need to be very small to comply with the hardware specifications

- End user/designer – graphics are also constrained in some cases to the expertise of the designer. Graphics will vary in terms of complexity depending upon whether a professional graphics designer or a user that dabbles for fun has created it.

Bitmap and vector graphics

Graphics can be divided into two main types:

- Bitmap
- Vector

Bitmap

Bitmap graphics are, also referred to as 'raster images', based on a grid of small squares that are referred to as pixels. Bitmap graphics represent subtle gradations of scales and colour as shown in Figure 7.15. Each pixel has an assigned location and colour value attached to it. This gradation of colour and scale provides excellent photographic or artwork created in painting software.

Figure 7.15
Enlarged bitmap

There are four main categories of bitmap graphics, these include:

(1) Line-art – these are images that contain only two colours, usually black and white
(2) Greyscale images – these contain some elements of grey blended in with the black and white
(3) Multitone images – these contain shades of two or more colours. The most popular multitone images are duotones, these usually consist of black and a second spot colour
(4) Full colour images – these contain a number of colour squares on the grid.

Vector graphics

Vector graphics are made up of mathematical definitions. Each individual line is made up of a number of points which are all connected, or a few control points that are connected using so-called Bezier curves as shown in Figure 7.16. The Bezier curve method usually generates the best results that are used by most drawing programs.

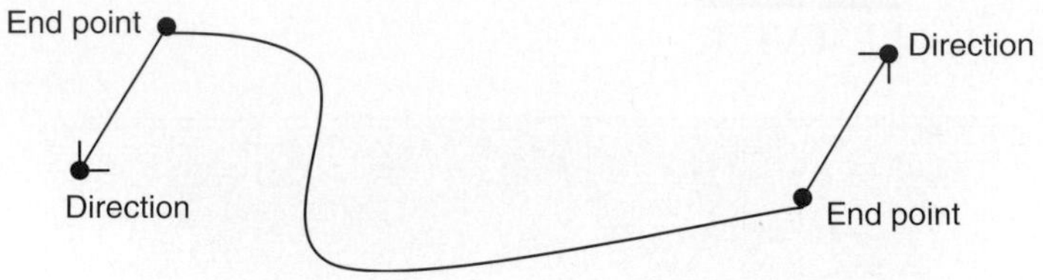

Figure 7.16

Sample Bezier curve

Vector images are very smooth and unlike bitmap images they do not distort as the shape changes, an example of a vector image can be seen in Figure 7.17.

Figure 7.17

Sample vector image

What does this mean?

Bezier curves

Bezier curves are used in computer graphics to produce curves which appear reasonably smooth at all scales.

Graphics tools and techniques

There are a number of ways that graphics can be generated, for example freehand drawings, the use of a device such as a camera, phone, web cam, scanner, etc. or by using specific software as referred to earlier.

When using a software package, there are a range of tools and techniques available to a user to change an original design into something completely different at the touch of a button.

Most graphics and drawing packages offer the same or very similar tools to enable a user to manipulate their design. Some of these will be illustrated using Serif DrawPlus. Figures 7.18–7.20 show the basic framework, tool bars and colour palette of the Serif DrawPlus package.

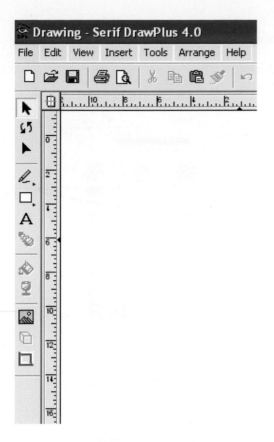

Figure 7.18

Serif DrawPlus tool and menu bar

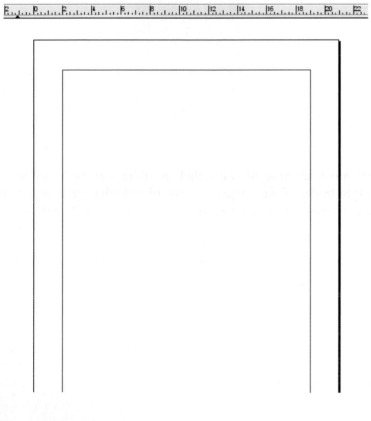

Figure 7.19

Serif DrawPlus drawing area

Figure 7.20

Serif DrawPlus colour palette

One of the ways to create a graphic using this piece of software is to select an object from the tool bar and place it within the drawing area.

Once a graphic has been designed, a number of tools and techniques can be used to change it, some of these will now be explored:

- Transparency tool
- Rotate and move
- Stencil effect
- Adding in a contour

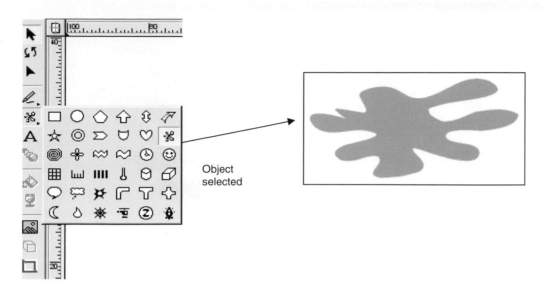

Object
selected

Figure 7.21
Serif DrawPlus – graphic

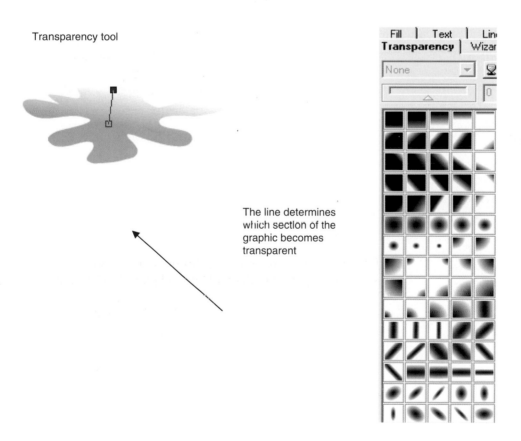

Transparency tool

The line determines
which section of the
graphic becomes
transparent

Figure 7.22
Using transparency

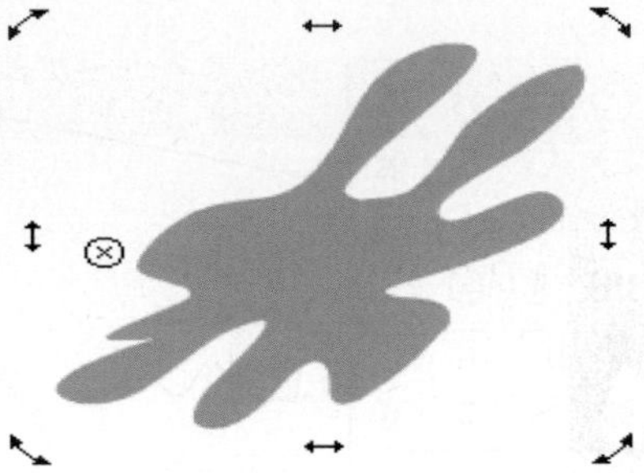

Figure 7.23
Using rotate and move

Figure 7.24
Stencil

Figure 7.25
Contouring

Using 'envelope wizard' the design and shape of a graphic can change
to match the selected envelope.

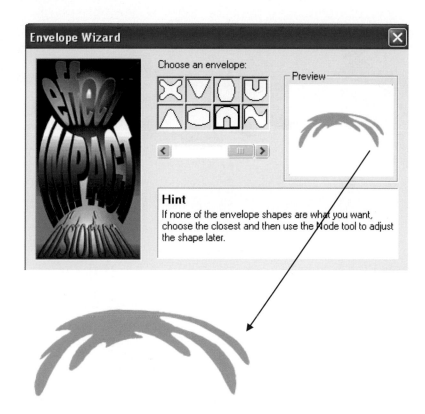

Figure 7.26
Using the envelope
feature

Curve toolbar – by moving over the curve points you can stretch and
distort the curves to make a new image.

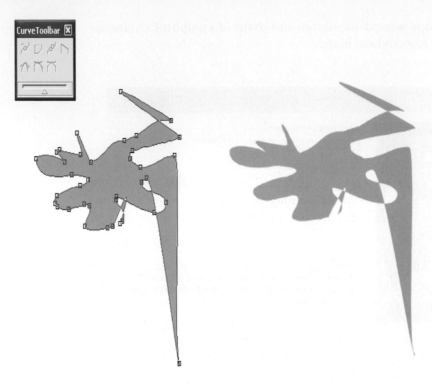

Figure 7.27

Using the curve feature

Other special effects such as sharpen, soften, smudge, distort, polarise, etc. can also be used to modify a graphic.

Activity 7

(a) Using a graphics/drawing package of your choice create a very simple image

(b) Save the image and then use a range of tools and techniques to manipulate the original image

(c) Each time you use a tool, save the image as a different version

(d) Once you have used about five different tools or techniques to manipulate your original image, produce an information sheet about the tools and techniques you have used, include screenshots of each of the revised images to support this.

Reviewing graphics

Once a graphic has been created, there are a number of checks or reviews that can be carried out to see whether or not the design meets the original requirement or target audience need.

The problem with graphics is that once you get into the design process it is very easy to stray from an original intention or concept because of the software tools available to change into something more complex or innovative.

Checking that the completed graphic still meets the objectives of the end user is crucial. The intention may be for the graphic to be simplistic and bold to use as a letterhead for example with no special effects required.

Another check that should be carried out is to see if the graphic and any associated text conveys the correct message. Does it include the corporate colours, is any accompanying text been proofread.

If the graphic has to be sent to other sources electronically, checks need to be put in place to ensure that it is in a suitable format, that it has been compressed and will actually send to another source or can be imported into another document.

Finally, reviews provided by the end user such as suggestions for improvement may be of use when considering another design.

Test your knowledge

(1) Why do you think it is important to review graphics?
(2) Do you think that this review/checking process should be carried out at the end of the design or continually throughout the design. Why do you think this?
(3) Identify three ways in which you can review graphics
(4) Why do you think that it is important for graphics to be in the correct file format?

Selecting, acquiring and importing images to enhance documents

There are a number of ways that images can be selected, acquired and imported to enhance a document. A large majority of word processing software applications have tools that enable a user to do this simply and effectively – see Figure 7.28.

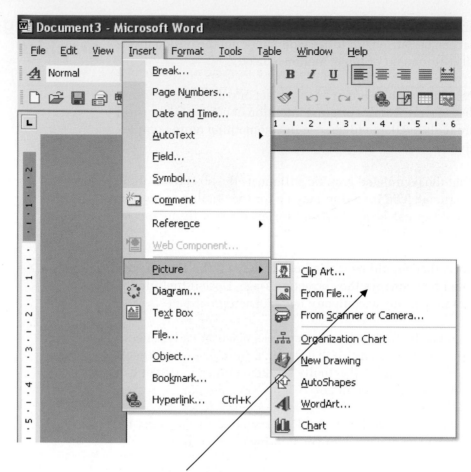

Ability to insert a picture via Clip Art, from a file or from a scanner or camera

Figure 7.28

Different ways of inserting images

There are a range of other ways that can be used to get graphics onto a document, some of these include:

• Downloading from another source, e.g. the Internet
• Scanning
• Importing from another source and cutting/copying and pasting.

Each of these methods although different in principle have the ability to source an image and move it from one destination to another.

Downloading from the Internet

Using images from the Internet in a document is very simple – by right-clicking on the image it will bring up a drop-down menu that gives you the option to 'save picture as' as shown in Figure 7.29. The picture can then be saved into an area for use at a later stage.

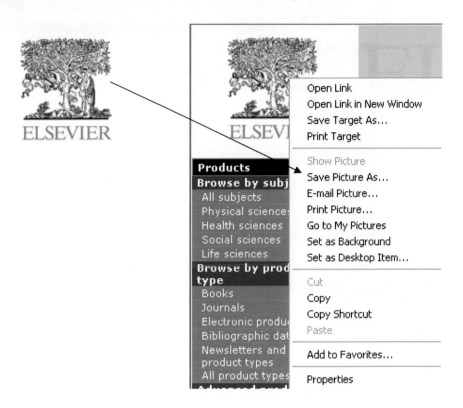

Figure 7.29
Saving a graphic from the Internet

Another way of taking images from the Internet or any other software package is to do what is known as a 'screen dump'. By pressing 'Ctrl' and 'PrtSc' together on a particular page, this will automatically capture that information. By using software such as 'Paint', the information can then be 'pasted' and cropped or edited to extract the required graphic or information as shown in Figure 7.30.

Scanning

Scanning images is very simple with the wide range of hardware that is available. A scanner is similar to a photocopier, it is a device that

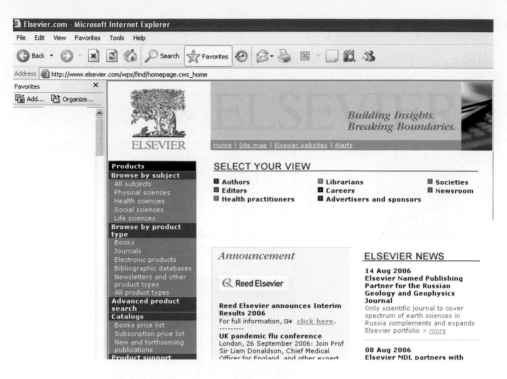

Figure 7.30

Screen dump of an entire web page

can read text or graphics from a document and can then translate this onto a computer through the use of compatible software. A scanner works by digitising the document/image and dividing the area into grids, each cell on the grid is then allocated a '0' or a '1' depending on whether or not that cell has been filled in.

Scanners differ in size and shape, you can have hand-held scanners that are moved across a page or flat-bed scanners where the document is placed on the 'bed'. There are also large sheet-fed scanners and overhead scanners.

Importing from another source and cutting/copying and pasting

Graphics can be brought into a document from another piece of software in a number of ways. Depending upon the type of application and the nature of the graphic it can be imported between applications, or if permitted it can be cut out and pasted into a document.

A good example of importing from one application to another is that
of Clip Art as shown in Figure 7.31.

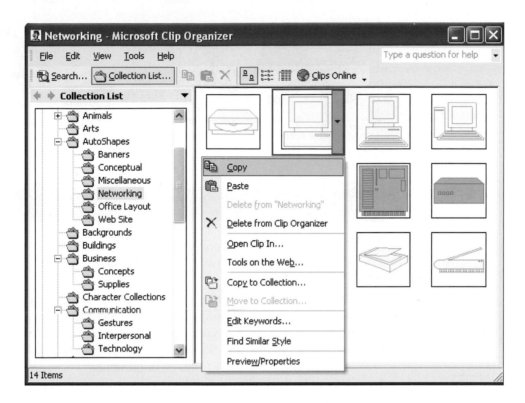

Figure 7.31

Using images from Clip Art

The images can then be used to enhance a document that has been
created as shown in Figure 7.32.

The One-Stop Computer Shop

14 Myers Lane
Hedgebrook
Norfolk
NR34 7TT

Figure 7.32

Use of graphics to
enhance a document

There are a number of ways that graphics can be used within a
document to enhance its content as shown in the following selection
of Figures 7.33–7.36.

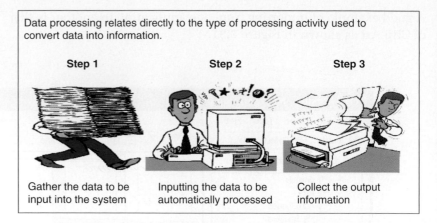

Data processing relates directly to the type of processing activity used to convert data into information.

Step 1	Step 2	Step 3
Gather the data to be input into the system	Inputting the data to be automatically processed	Collect the output information

Figure 7.33

Graphics used to enhance a set of instructions

Activity 8

Graphics can be used to enhance a document and can be sourced from a number of packages, devices and applications.

(a) Using at least three different methods (downloading, copying and pasting, screen dump, importing, scanning, etc.). Obtain a graphic and store it in your documents/pictures for future use

(b) Once you have stored the three separate graphics, use them to enhance three different types of documents

(c) State which method of obtaining the graphic you found the easiest and why

(d) Provide a list of five other purposes that a graphic could be used for to enhance a document.

Editing acquired images

When using images the process of transferring them from one source to another may be relatively straightforward, however, in order to use the graphic to enhance a document some editing may have to take place to ensure that it fits the purpose for which it is intended. For example, a graphic that is inserted into a letterhead to act as a logo, may need to be resized to make it small enough to fit within the required header of the letter etc.

Menu

Starters

French onion soup

with croutons

Melon with fruit coulis

Main

Poached salmon with a herb sauce

Roast beef

Mushroom risotto

Dessert

Chocolate torte

Fresh fruit salad

Coffee and mints

Figure 7.34

Graphics used to enhance a menu

AGENDA

Staff Committee Meeting

Tuesday 15 August 2006
Room 5 First Floor

1 Re-structuring programme
2 Appointment of new Section Leader
3 Retirement party for J. Norson
4 New canteen facilities
5 Staff outing proposals
6 Any other issues

Figure 7.35

Graphics to enhance
a business document

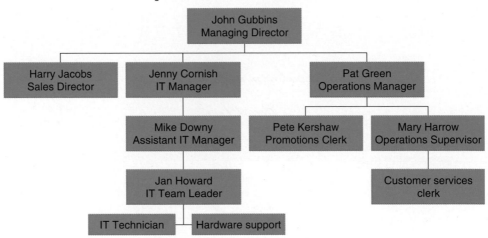

Organisation Chart for Gubbins Hardware

Figure 7.36

Graphic illustrating the structure of personnel within an organisation

There are a number of editing features that can be used to manipulate
a graphic, some of these include:

- Resizing, flipping, rotating
- Colour correction
- Text wrapping
- Positioning

Resizing, flipping and rotating

Resizing, flipping and rotating an object is very easy to do with any
drawing package that has the tools to facilitate this. Images can be
resized and angles altered at the click of a button.

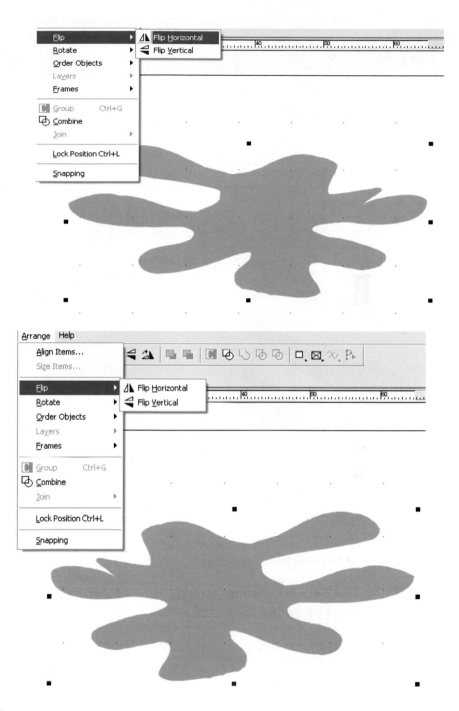

Figure 7.37
Horizontal flipping

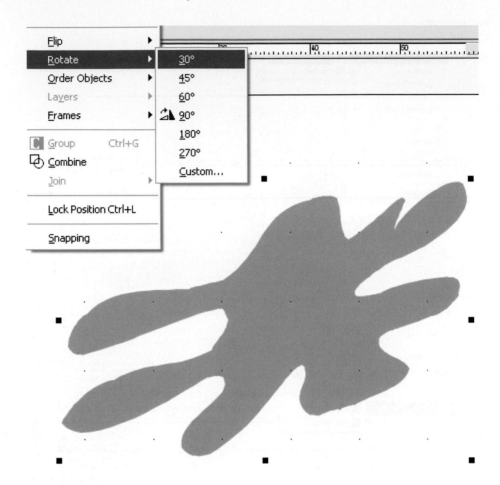

Figure 7.38
Rotating an object

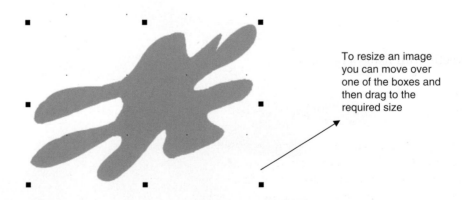

Figure 7.39
Resizing an image

Colour correction

Colour correction/filling is very easy to apply to an object. By selecting the 'spray can', 'brush' or other colour tool and clicking on the image or section of the image, you can then select a 'fill' design and an appropriate colour that will then be applied to your image.

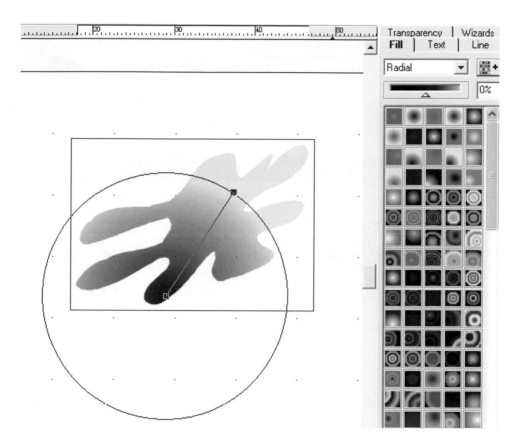

Figure 7.40
Colour correction/fill using a radial design

Text wrapping

Text can be added and wrapped around an image to support the design or provide a written explanation of the graphic. Text wrapping can be created in many ways using a 'wordart' tool, a built in text box tool or by positioning the graphic in such a way that text can be wrapped around either side, above and below as shown in Figure 7.41.

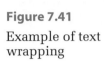

Figure 7.41

Example of text wrapping

This is to demonstrate how text can be wrapped around a specific image. By formatting the graphics layout you can select an option as shown in Figure 7.42 that will enable text to be moulded around an object.

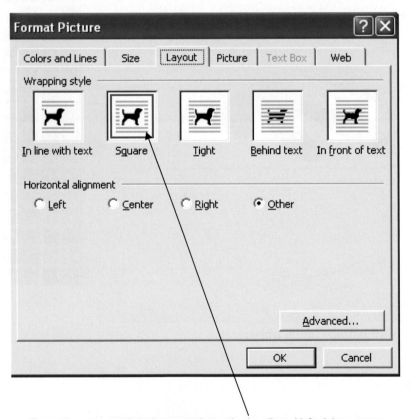

Text will wrap around the image and can also be aligned left, right or centre.

Figure 7.42

Text alignment

Text will wrap around the image and can also be aligned left, right or centre.

Positioning a graphic

Positioning a graphic on a page is very simple in terms of wherever the cursor is, the graphic will be introduced. However, once the graphic is on the page you may have to adjust its size and position so that it fits in with the rest of the document. By formatting the graphic layout as shown in Figure 7.42 you then have the flexibility to move the graphic to its desired location.

There is certain legislation that offers protection to original authors and designers that have their work in the public domain (in books, magazines, journals, on the Internet, etc.). This legislation is referred to as the Copyright, Designs and Patents Act (1988).

Copyright legislation

Copyright, Designs and Patents Act (1988)

The Copyright, Designs and Patents Act provides protection to software developers and organisations against unauthorised copying of their software, designs, printed material and any other product. Under copyright legislation, an organisation or developer can ensure that its Intellectual Property Rights (IPR) has been safeguarded against third parties who wish to exploit and make gains from the originator's research and developments.

What does this mean?

Intellectual Property Rights: refers to patents, registered designs and design rights, registered trade marks and copyright.

Index